Battlegr

BEAUCOURT

Battleground Europe

BEAUCOURT

Michael Renshaw

Series editor
Nigel Cave

LEO COOPER

First published in 2003 by
LEO COOPER
an imprint of
Pen & Sword Books Limited
47 Church Street, Barnsley, South Yorkshire S70 2AS

ISBN 0 85052 853 4

A CIP catalogue of this book is available
from the British Library

Printed by CPI UK

*For up-to-date information on other titles produced under the Leo Cooper imprint,
please telephone or write to:*

Pen & Sword Books Ltd, FREEPOST, 47 Church Street
Barnsley, South Yorkshire S70 2AS
Telephone 01226 734222

CONTENTS

Introduction by Series Editor.. 6
Author's Introduction... 7
The Somme battlefield today... 10

Chapter 1 **Saturday 1 July**.. 16
Chapter 2 **Sunday 3 September**....................................... 36
Chapter 3 **Monday 13 November**..................................... 50
Chapter 4 **Attack of 39 Division 13 November**.................. 77
Chapter 5 **Tuesday 14 November**.................................... 85
Chapter 6 **Visiting the battlefields**................................ 95

  Walk 1: **Attack of the 9 Royal Irish Fusiliers and
         12 Royal Irish Rifles**.......................... 106
  Walk 2: **Attack of 3 September and 13 November**........ 113
  Walk 3: **The German front line**................................. 117
  Walk 4: **The Green Line**... 127

Chapter 11 **There is a Green Hill far away**....................... 142
Chapter 12 **The Cemeteries**.. 146
Chapter 13 **A short tour of the Somme**........................... 151
Chapter 14 **And afterwards**.. 154

Index.. 157
Acknowledgements... 160

Section of map of area within which the book is based.

Introduction by the Series Editor

Beaucourt is a quiet and sleepy place, snoozing gently by the lazy Ancre. It is hard to imagine that it could ever have been the scene of such ferocious fighting as that which took place here in November 1916, in the dying throes of the Battle of the Somme. The battle here reveals something about the improvement in the capability of the British army in the field: men were more willing to take the initiative, systems were more flexible, the use of weapons had improved - all the consequence of the ghastly (and, of course, ghastly for both sides, a point often ignored) grinding battles which taught lessons in a terrible and unforgiving way.

Although Beaucourt is best remembered for the fighting in that gloomy, sodden and cold November (and in personality terms, remembered for the VC won by Bernard Freyberg), there was fighting along the northern bank of the Ancre prior to this. Most especially the action of a brigade of the 36th (Ulster) Division on 1st July is often forgotten; perhaps because it was as unsuccessful as the attacks of the other British formations north of the Ancre on that fateful day. Certainly it did not have the same possibilities of the extraordinary advances, though lost, by the two sister brigades south of the river.

The November fighting before Beaucourt is an action where good observation of the ground may be had from north and south, which does much to help in understanding the battle; but nothing can replace walking the ground and spotting those dips and folds, those hidden gullies, which made what looks so deceptively easy from a distance in fact a tremendous struggle, when ingenuity and fortitude was displayed in equal measure by two highly committed sides.

Michael Renshaw leads the tourer around the battlefield with a deft touch, coming from years of knowing this ground so well, based as he is with a house just the other side of the hill. Knowledge of the ground is accompanied by extensive work in the archives, which combines to produce a well balanced account of the fighting here and a useful addition to the Somme battle literature.

It is unlikely that any of the battlefield visitors will be walking the area in the same weather conditions as much of the fighting, especially that of November 1916, but following the tours should enable all of us to have a greater understanding of the problems that faced all ranks of the armies; and that is surely a reasonable achievement.

Nigel Cave
Porta Latina, Rome

AUTHOR'S INTRODUCTION

During a discussion about the Great War, an acquaintance of mine remarked that 'World War One goes on and on.' Somewhat puzzled I pressed him further . 'Well, he continued, we all sit around reliving and re-fighting the battles and usually end up disagreeing about it all.' Certainly, if one single event in the twentieth century generates more controversy and affects more people, even today, I must confess I haven't heard of it.

Difficult, at times, though it may be, this place is not an appropriate one to consider or develop personal opinions and theories on what went wrong (or for that matter what went right). We are concerned only in finding out and attempting to discover what actually happened. However, as Douglas Jerrold (on whose writings some of this book has been based) pointed out, what really happened can never wholly be known for many reasons. Those charged with recording events at the battlefront were often wounded and killed and never got to produce their reports. Those that did survive relied on accounts from officers and men and these often varied in their detail with the result that it is not difficult to travel through all the diaries and reports today and find conflicting and contradictory accounts of the same situation.

Those that survived the sinking of the *Titanic* later gave witness at the resulting enquiries and their accounts were also widely published. In the horror and shock of their experience, descriptions of exactly how the doomed vessel went to the bottom of the sea varied widely. Although everyone must have seen exactly the same dramatic event;

Winter on the Somme.

recollected at a later date, for whatever reason, genuine witness was divided. So one's search for the truth may never be satisfied and we can only be guided by what has been spoken of and written before and where there is divergence we can only make our own minds up. Every grave we visit and every name on a memorial not only has a story of tragedy and bereavement attached to it but, for the most part, an untold story, perhaps of bad luck or indeed heroism. A popular belief still held strongly by some is of courageous Tommies fighting to ultimate victory over a dehumanised enemy but with the handicap of being led by ineffective generals and senior officers. This, of course, is the 'Lions led by Donkeys' syndrome, a term attributed to General Luddendorff of the German High Command in his description of the British Army in 1914. Of course in reality every soldier who went to war was not a hero and equally every officer was not a bungling idiot. However, as already stated, this is not the place to express too many opinions and theories.

One of the most difficult things which confronts an author attempting to write about the First World War is how to convey the reality of it all. So many of the men who were actually there and returned never spoke of what they had seen and experienced. Possibly they could not find the words to describe it all, even if they wanted to. It was an experience that could only, in truth, be shared by those who were there. To read the matter-of-fact reports and diaries written at the time only serves to disguise the horror.

There do not seem to be the available words in the English language that can adequately illustrate the reality, although through some of the

A casualty near Beaumont Hamel.

poetry we are able to share some of this.

This book, then, is essentially a sanitised version of what happened. The words such as 'mud', 'cold' and 'wounded' fail to adequately translate into what it really meant. Sometimes I walk, shivering in the bitter cold and rain, on my way home at night, thinking of the warm bed that awaits at the termination of a short journey and also thinking of the men who, already soaked through and standing in deep mud, having not slept for perhaps forty-eight hours, awaited their fate in an attack due to take place at dawn. In one small way it is the nearest that I can get to it.

The book is also a one-sided version of events. Little is recorded here of the German experience for, although much exists, it is hard to access and written in German, obviously. There are some examples translated but, in any case, it would necessitate curtailing some of the British records to fit it all in and it is this record that is the primary purpose of the book. However, it should be remembered that the German soldiers were very fine troops, but had the disadvantage of fighting on foreign soil and were usually outnumbered. The defeat of Germany was only brought about by an alliance of numerous countries and even then in 1918 they so very nearly pulled it off, they just ran out of manpower.

The First World War changed the nature of British society. Before the war, the 'ruling classes' were considered omnipotent, unchallengeable, and of course they knew what was best. However war does not discriminate on behalf of the privileged, they suffer, die and are affected by fear and their decision making process is as affected by overpowering stress and ignorance as the next man. The myth was stripped away and after the war the erosion of the class system had begun.

Second Lieutenant Harold Macmillan, Grenadier Guards.

Probably one of the best illustrations of this is shown in the story of Harold Macmillan, a young lieutenant in the Grenadier Guards, who lay alone and wounded in a shell hole near Guillemont in the Somme battle. Shells crashed around and as he lapsed in and out of consciousness he hoped he would not be buried alive by the fall-out of the shelling. He passed the time and awaited his fate reading his book of Greek prose which he carried with him. Suddenly a figure appeared over the lip of the shell hole. It was one of his sergeants, Company

9

Sergeant Major Norton, who, correctly standing to attention roared above the din of the guns, 'Thank you, sir, for leave to carry you away!' The future prime minister never forgot that 'splendid fellow' and all the men he was thrown into contact with in the trenches. After the war he entered politics and stood for Parliament at Stockton-on-Tees, an unfashionable North Eastern constituency. In his memoirs and in his last speech in the House of Lords he wrote and spoke warmly of the men and of his experiences with them. Wounded three times, the subsequent limp hand shake, and that shuffling walk provided material for satire when he became prime minister. The Somme may have been Harold Macmillan's 'Damascus' but his newly found attitudes and values alienated him from the aristocratic family into which he had married.

Auchonvillers, Somme 2003

THE SOMME BATTLEFIELDS TODAY

There are many visitors today to the Western Front. In recent years the growth in numbers not only to the Somme Département, but to many other sections of the 400 miles of trenches that existed between the English Channel and the French/Swiss border, has been remarkable. The reasons for this are many and varied but one event which has had as much an influence on this migration as any other was the publication of a book aptly entitled *Before Endeavours Fade* by the late Rose Coombs MBE, who was employed at the Imperial War Museum. This publication in the seventies was the forerunner to many and more prolific authors and some, perhaps, better known. Rose's book, though, set many off in the right direction (even if on occasion the map showed it otherwise!). But even with its minor imperfections, a huge chunk of credit must go to Rose Coombs for what we enjoy today.

The Cross of Sacri

I used to say to my friends, 'I'm off to the Western Front', but came to realise that I was looking for a place that did not exist anymore. While the 'Western Front' certainly was a place with an historical geography, it was, probably more than anything, a physical experience, a state of mind exclusive to those who went there at the time and we can never share that nor the geography either. It has all but disappeared under buildings, motorways and the plough. We can trace its course on the old maps but all this now belongs to another generation. It is someone's potato field, someone's garden, a supermarket or autoroute. We have no ownership of it in any sense except the historical. Ever since my first visit to the Somme in 1986, much that had been left has also disappeared. The vagaries of the European Common Agricultural Policy has played its part. Farmers have ploughed as much ground as possible to obtain higher subsidies which has resulted in the destruction of numerous little corners; bits of woodland, hedges, quarries and suchlike that had been wisely left untouched by previous generations who remembered that there was an old munitions dump or other site of dubious history there. But more of that later. Such is progress and the visitor will find little of the world inhabited by the men of 1914-18.

The Somme battlefields are pleasantly rural, the villages built of red brick are unprepossessing and it has to be remembered that none have a history of longer than about seventy five years. Rebuilding the destroyed villages commenced in the late twenties in earnest, although pre-fabricated huts and chalets appeared before this time, some of which are still inhabited today. This book takes its name from the Beaucourt village situated in the Ancre valley, and should not be confused with other Beaucourts in the Somme area. A further few words of explanation are needed here. Some of the other villages in the area where this book is set have often confused the visitor by the way they are named. Traditionally there was Beaumont-Hamel, Beaucourt-Hamel, Hamel and Beaucourt sur Ancre. The first three places named form one commune with one mayor. Beaumont, having the largest population, takes precedence and therefore has the name of Hamel attached to it. Hamel stands in its own right but the nearest village to the station is Beaucourt and is named as such. However it is actually in the commune of Hamel, hence Beaucourt-Hamel. Then there is Beaucourt sur Ancre which is independent of them all! All this continued until fairly recently when it was observed that the village signs in Beaumont-Hamel, which are quite often damaged by agricultural vehicles, were being replaced with just 'Beaumont' and Beaucourt-Hamel is now known as 'Beaucourt Gare' [except that it is now closed!]. Beaucourt sur Ancre is now grammatically correct as Beaucourt sur l'Ancre.

I am sure that as far as the history is concerned though, Beaumont-Hamel will always remain and be remembered as one of the most feared and famous names on the battlefield and as such is carved on many a memorial and recorded in many a book.

Gunfire can still be heard on the Somme battlefields. The French thirst for '*La Chasse*' (the hunt) is as unquenched as ever and from

September onwards through to the spring, care must be taken, especially at weekends. All woodland is private on the Somme and should not be entered unless permission has been obtained. Even if you are tempted to take a little stroll into an unfenced wood, where history beckons, be careful; there are traps and the 'shooters', as we call them, inhabit the woods – officially from January onwards, but unofficially at other times too.

Access to the countryside is not normally a problem. Unless there is a notice to the contrary (*Interdit*) or the ground is fenced, it is possible to walk on the fields, subject, of course, to any growing crops. In the right location and at the right time, that is after rain has washed out the ploughing, it is possible to pick up a few 'souvenirs' from the debris of war still coming to the surface. Naturally, it is foolish to meddle with anything that is or looks explosive. Shells and grenades seem much less frequent than in previous years, at least in the Somme area, but those that remain are just as lethal potentially. I know, there are many, both French and English, who will tell you they have handled many items of unexploded ordnance, even defused some, but some have also been casualties.

An English friend of mine living near Reninghelst, Belgium, told me some years ago of the villager who thought he would have a meddle with an unusual shell that he had found and which he kept in his garden shed, while his family went to Sunday morning Mass. It started to fizz and he literally ran for his life. It took the back of his house out complete with Sunday dinner! I wonder what he said to his wife?

In one sense the Somme consists of two things. It is both a massive graveyard and an abandoned munitions dump. If you are nervous or uncertain about either, then it is probably better not to go. As with the unexploded shells and grenades, there were also many undiscovered bodies of French, German and British soldiers and the Somme is still giving up its dead. In addition to this, it is not uncommon to find the fragmented remains of those unfortunate to have been blown up by explosion, somebody's boy who simply disappeared. The temptation to go and dig up the Somme, should be strongly resisted. First of all, it is against the law to use a metal detector, although there is evidence that this sub culture is alive and well among certain groups of both French and the British visitors.

The debris of war.

12

Secondly, it creates much damage and mess. Thirdly, it can be dangerous. By all means have a scratch around on a bank or under a friendly farmer's hedge, but serious excavation is best left to the farmer, builder or pipe layer who with a bit of 'bribery' and 'international sign language' will willingly part with all they can find, for a few Euros, if it's a bit of (safe) memorabilia you are after.

The most tangible element of the Western Front that we can visit today consists of the cemeteries and memorials. These sites mark the place where it all happened and today we can see the result of all the work of the then Imperial War Graves Commission, led by Sir Fabian Ware, who created what we see. The work goes on and the 'Flagship' of the Somme is the massive 'Memorial to the Missing' at Thiepval, designed by Sir Edward Lutyens and dedicated in 1932 by the Prince of Wales, later Edward VIII of abdication controversy. This bears the name of approximately 73,000 men lost in battle who have no known grave.The cemeteries are tended by teams of gardeners who rotate around their 'group' from a nearby workbase. The maintenance of the walls, headstones and buildings is directed from the headquarters of the Commonwealth War Graves Commission at Beaurains, south of Arras. Their work, it hardly needs to be stated, is of the highest standard and much appreciated.

I commenced this introduction by mentioning Rose Coombs. I was fortunate to meet her twice. On my first visit to Ypres in November 1986, I was befriended by a member of the Ypres Branch of the Royal British Legion who took me and my daughter, Emma, to a social event in St George's Church Hall.

I sat in a small group and later an impressive lady joined us, chatting to people she knew. It was Rose Coombs. I already had her book, but not with me for signing, unfortunately. It was my turn to buy a round of drinks which I carried around on a tray. A year passed and I was again at the same annual social. Again Rose Coombs was present and spoke with my friends during the course of the evening. As previously I rose to replenish the empty glasses on the table. 'Sit down' the formidable figure boomed, 'I seem to remember it's my round!'

War Graves equipment at New Munich Trench.

GERMAN ARMY ORGANISATION

A brief and simplified version of the German Army is given as it existed in 1914.

A corps had two infantry divisions and seven other sections, which for the purposes of this book, we shall put to one side. An infantry division consisted of two brigades, one artillery brigade and three or four squadrons of cavalry. An infantry brigade was subdivided into two regiments and each regiment had three battalions numbered I II and III and a machine gun company. Each battalion then comprised four companies, similar to their British counterparts.

A company at full strength would have numbered five officers and 259 men organised into three platoons each with four sections, making twelve in all and numbered 1-12. Normally all three battalions were kept together and so a German regiment was about the same as a British brigade.

Identification of German troops were given in reverse order, thus: battalion number I II or III, regiment number and division number. Hence:

III/95 Regiment/38 Division.

German machine gun team.

BRITISH ARMY ORGANISATION

An abridged version is given here to assist the reader follow the battle narrative.

An army consists of a number of corps, which, in turn are made up of divisions, which was normally commanded by a major general. A division in the British Army has three brigades. In the 1914-1918 war a brigade was commanded by a brigadier general.

Until early 1918 each brigade contained four infantry battalions making a total of twelve plus one pioneer battalion. A battalion would be under the direction of a lieutenant colonel, with a major as second in command. The adjutant would normally be a captain or lieutenant. The total strength of a battalion would be just over one thousand, although this was rarely achieved. Each battalion also had a machine gun section with a lieutenant in command, and a support section with signallers and stretcher bearers etc.

Leaving aside the details of the headquarters staff and moving to the more relevant information for the purposes of this book, the assaulting troops were divided into four companies, each commanded by a major or a captain and a captain or lieutenant as second in command. Each company was divided into four platoons, each commanded by a lieutenant or second lieutenant, making a total of six officers. Each platoon was subdivided into four sections. They were under the command of a sergeant or other non commisioned officer. Headquarters staff were also attached to each company.

The numbers in an infantry battalion varied enormously. To look at approximate numbers, we will work upwards from section level and here we are looking at men that were likely to be going into action.

A section commander would expect to have up to fourteen men and, therefore, a platoon could be in excess of fifty and a company becomes about two hundred.

However, these are theoretical figures and in the November 1916 a company was more likely to be nearer one hundred and twenty-five. In July many of the British battalions went into action with between 700 and 800 men.

Chapter One

SATURDAY 1 JULY 1916

The village of Beaucourt sur l'Ancre lies on the north bank of the River Ancre in the Département of the Somme. The river is a small but pretty tributary of the Somme River and continues its journey onward to join its more notable counterpart at Corbie, a pleasant town with a fine abbey. The Somme River itself was in the French sector during the battles of 1916 and the Ancre provided the fulcrum across which the British made their assault.

Beaucourt was one of the villages just behind the German main position that was part of the line of defence against the British which was to prove very effective. The British trench system by comparison was inferior. The position inherited from the French in June 1915 was

Map 1: Scale 1:10000. The Ulster Division on the north bank of the Ancre 1 July 1916. This map is taken from the 29th Division records. It denotes that the salient of Mary Redan was in their sector but no attempt was made to assault from that position. The 29th Division kept to the left. Also the trench referred to as New Trench and used by the 12/Royal Irish Fusiliers, is shown here as Regent Street and Whitehall.

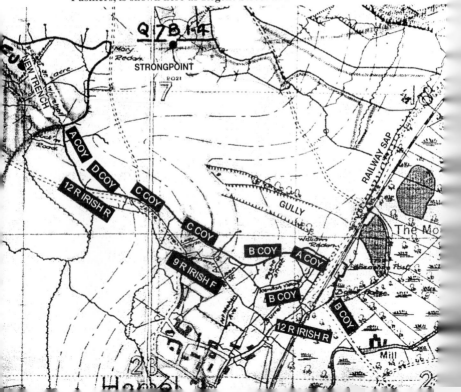

largely based on the location where the French held up the German advance and was a haphazard arrangement with no thought given to position or the military strategy of the time either in defence or attack. Furthermore, in the following twelve months during which the area was a quiet sector, the Germans had little to do but dig and dig they did, with great effect, utilising the many cave systems deep in the chalk and converting them into huge underground barracks, hospitals and munitions dumps. Where there were no caves, they dug anyway, sometimes thirty or forty feet down. So while the Germans perfected their positions, the British recruited and hurriedly trained its volunteer army, but did little to improve the positions they held, although it could be argued that attack, not defence, was uppermost in their minds.

Time and again, reading the reports and diaries of the battles, it is recorded that the British soldiers found themselves attacking 'from half dug trenches.'

This book is concerned with the major attacks that took place in the immediate vicinity of the River Ancre in front of Beaucourt sur l'Ancre, from 1 July through to November 1916 with the greater detail being devoted to the north bank. Saturday 1 July 1916 dawned bright and clear after days of inclement weather which had delayed the British offensive which was intended to draw the fire of the German Army away from Verdun. The French were under intense pressure and Sir Douglas Haig was, in turn, pressurised into making an attack with largely inexperienced volunteers on ground he

Some of the unexploded shells.

British artillery in action.

did not favour. Much preparation went into the battle plan and the key to success was to be in the hands of the artillery. A barrage of huge proportions was devised which was to smash the German defences and thus provide the inexperienced troops with a simplified objective. 1,513 field guns were placed, on average, every twenty yards with a heavy gun every sixty yards. Inexplicably, though, among those things overlooked was the existence of the deep dugouts within which the Germans sheltered in considerable number and comfort. Although one of these had been captured by the French not far away, the significance of this apparently was not sufficiently recognised. Add to this that the wrong kind of shells were used to attempt to cut the wire in front of the German trenches and too many of the shells failed to explode (it is estimated that out of 1,628,000 shells fired, one third failed to detonate), and it is easy to see, with hindsight, the impending disaster of 1 July 1916.

However, prior to all this, spirits had been generally high and there was some optimism. On the north bank of the Ancre on the night of 30 June men of the 36th (Ulster) Division gathered in the crowded communication trenches and in the village of Hamel just behind the front line. They comprised half of the 108 Brigade, the 9/Royal Irish Fusiliers (Armagh, Monaghan and Cavan Volunteers) and the 12/Royal Irish Rifles (Mid Antrim Volunteers). The 9/Royal Irish Fusiliers consisted of many men of rural origin from Armagh and who worked in agricultural occupations. The battalion was commanded by Colonel

Soldiers moving up through Hamel village.

Stewart W Blacker, a much respected figure from that area, and were nicknamed 'Blackers Boys.'

'I was a sniper in the 9th Fusiliers, Blackers Boys, the best trained men in the British Army. We moved up on the day before 30th June... I was sent down to the dugout for a sleep but the noise of the mortars kept me awake. When it was daylight we moved out to the trenches and had a bite to eat. There was a fellow Hobbs from Lurgan and would you believe it, he was shaving. When he was finished he took out a clean pair of socks and put them on just as if he was back in barracks. Anyway we moved up under our barrage... As it lifted we were in and through the German lines before they could recover. There was this big ditch – the gorge [Gully] that runs at right angles to the river and this was wired, but up near us the wire was well cut and our lot and the ones that followed got through. The next lot got caught by the machine guns away up on our left.'

The British front line here lay on an exposed ridge to the south-west of the village of Beaucourt. On the right flank between the attacking troops and the German front line lay a steep gully that ran from the Hamel - Beaucourt road and gradually became less deep as it progressed north towards the extreme left flank. On the right flank, the Paris - Lille railway track ran alongside this road. Beyond that was the River Ancre and a series of lakes and marshy ground over which it was not possible to dig any trenches or defensive positions as everything just filled up with water. On the extreme left hand flank, the Divisional boundary joined with that of the 29/Division at a small salient known as Mary Redan, an exposed position over a flatter terrain with no natural cover (see map 1). At 7.20am the great mine exploded on the nearby Hawthorn Ridge which only served to alert the Germans in the opposing trenches.

'There was a wee runt of a man with us from Ballymena. Even when standing on a box he could hardly see over the parapet, but a powerful hard wee man he was and he was wearing what you would call nowadays an old fashioned sash. Somebody shouted at him "Whet's that yer wearing Jimmie?" "Ye idiot ye, did ye know nothing? It's the first of July, the day William fought and won the Boyne. That's our Boyne over there', he said pointing to the river below. "Give us a song," someone shouted. He struck up with 'July the first in Oldbridge town' You never hear it sung now but we all knowed it and we sung it even over the shelling that was going on. A couple of hours later I saw him lying dead with his

bayonet stuck through a big German officer twice his size. The German still had his pistol in his hand he killed Jimmie with.'

'I'm sure you've heard of men going in with shouts of 'no surrender' and things like that when they formed up in no mans land. It's hard to say what happened or what anybody said there's so much noise you could hardly hear the whistles going. But I do know one officer, from the West Belfast UVF, Major G H Gaffikin led his men over waving an orange coloured handkerchief.'

In talking to survivors of the Great War and in particular to those who had experienced the ultimate test of courage of going 'over the top', knowing that you presented the enemy with a fairly simple target, many have put down their survival to the fact that they were in the first wave. The Germans, deep in their dugouts had to emerge from these shelters and bring their machine guns with them in pieces. Furthermore, the actual front lines were often (but not always) thinly defended, sometimes with only lookout posts. The real threat came from the second and third line system of trenches where fortified machine gun positions were established.

The dispositions of 108 Brigade are as detailed on Map 1. The best way of describing what happened is by starting on the left flank and taking each company in turn. The front line British trench in this sector was approached by a long communication trench named New Trench. On the extreme left of the attack, A Company of the 12/Royal Irish Rifles was in touch with the 29th Division and they formed up in the sunken road in advance of the front line trench. At zero hour Number 4 Platoon led the attack and were immediately fired on heavily by machine guns. They were closely followed by Number 3 Platoon, who, finding gaps in the wire, made for the German front line. However there was a strongpoint in a salient in the German line from where three or four machine guns enfiladed the gaps and both platoons took

The sunken road near Mary Redan. The Thiepval Memorial can be seen centre in the background.

heavy casualties. Another two machine guns were also active each side of the main gap in the wire and in addition the platoon were attacked by a German bombing party. Lieutenant W McCluggage collected what men had made it into the German front line and attempted to rush the second line, but he was shot dead in the attempt and the attack fell back. The second line was full of German troops who fired on Number 1 and 2 Platoons as they also tried to advance to the German front line. The Germans also attacked those already there and stood right up on top of the parapets and threw stick grenades. Lieutenant T G Haughton was wounded in the leg leading his platoon but carried on. The machine-gun fire was extremely heavy, but the battle continued until an order to retire was given. Lieutenant Haughton was killed in the retirement and the remnants of all four platoons took cover in the sunken road. Second Lieutenant Dickson was the only officer left and he ordered another advance. He was immediately wounded very severely as the men were met again with terrific fire from the strongpoint. He carried on but eventually fell. Another retirement was made and Rifleman McMullan, who was the only man left of his Lewis gun crew, was also the last man away in the retreat, but not before he bravely put the Lewis gun to his shoulder and fired two magazines into the German second line and then, dodging the bullets, made it safely back to New Trench with his gun.

On the immediate right of A Company, D Company befell a similar fate. The attack was led by Sir Harry MacNaghten, Bart and Sergeant McFall with Number 16 Platoon and initially the German front line was penetrated. Sergeant McFall found some dugouts and ordered them to be bombed. The Germans in the second line again stood up and threw bombs into the front line and fired on the successive advancing platoons.

When the order to retire was shouted, Sir Harry got out of the trench to countermand this but was immediately shot at close range through his legs by a machine gun and he fell back into the trench. Rifleman Kane, who was with Sir Harry, rushed the machine gun and bayoneted the German responsible. A later account given by Rifleman Galloway, who was lying wounded in a nearby shell hole at the same time, reported that he saw Sir Harry lying on top of the parapet of the German trench, when three Germans advanced to take Sir Harry prisoner. They were attacked by a man of his regiment with his bayonet but he was killed and the Germans carried the officer away.

Second Lieutenant Sir E H MacNaghten, 6th Bart. 1 Black Watch, attached 12 Royal Irish Fusiliers, aged twenty, is commemorated on the Thiepval Memorial.

German troops counterattack with stick grenades.

Sir Harry was never seen again. This brave defence of Sir Harry is probably not the same as that undertaken by Rifleman Kane, as no soldier of that name was killed in the battalion that day.

Next in line, C Company went forward before zero hour and immediately came under fire from machine guns. Number 10 Platoon led the attack followed by Number 11 Platoon. There were only two small gaps in the wire and Number 10 Platoon split into two, each half going for a gap, although there was a German machine gun trained on each one. Even so, some men succeeded in getting into the German front line. Number 11 Platoon repeated the effort and under intense fire a few more men got through. Captain Griffiths collected 9 and 12 Platoons together and gave the order to charge but he was killed. Soon afterwards the order to retire was given but Sergeant Connaughan, Corporal Herbison and Lance Corporal Jackson stayed and fired at the Germans who were still standing on their parapets throwing stick bombs and they were able to inflict some casualties.

There were very many casualties and already few men of the battalion left, but another attack was ordered for 10.12am. All available men from all the attacking companies were amalgamated. Only about one hundred assembled and were led into the attack by Major C G Cole-Hamilton. Sergeant McFall (D Company), Sergeant A Smith and Lance Corporal W Harvey (C Company) were exceptionally cool and skilful in leading the attack, which was made under heavy shrapnel shelling and was met with more intense machine-gun fire. It never reached the German front line. A third attack was ordered for 12.30pm and every available man was assembled in New Trench. This time the total was only forty-six. The men went forward and were lying out under the cover of the sunken road when Major Cole-Hamilton called off the attack, seeing that it was useless. Such a small force could not possibly make any progress and this was confirmed by Lieutenant Colonel S Bull, the commanding officer.

From the foregoing it seems that no lodgement was made in the German second line and that machine-gun fire was the biggest factor, in spite of the determined and brave efforts of the men of the 12/Royal Irish Rifles. So before midday it was, effectively, all over. By 2.00pm all those capable of falling back into New Trench had returned. Only those out wounded and stricken in No Man's Land were left. Later, work commenced in earnest to try and relieve the plight of those so unfortunate. Among those actively engaged in this sorry occupation was Private R Quigg. He worked for Sir Harry MacNaghten on his estate in Bushmills and, unaware of Sir Harry's capture, went out to search for him. Seven times he went out and each time returned with a wounded man, eventually giving up owing to sheer exhaustion. He was subsequently awarded the Victoria Cross.

We move now further to the right and look at the attack of the 9/Royal Irish Fusiliers who also had B Company of the 12/Royal Irish Rifles attached to their right flank.

As with the 12/Royal Irish Rifles, the 9/Royal Irish Fusiliers had moved into position on the night of 30 June/1 July. They had fifteen officers and approximately 600 other ranks. No special assembly trenches had been dug and the two leading waves assembled in the front line on a four platoon front. On the right next to the railway line and river, was A Company, commanded by Captain C Ensor. Right centre, B Company was led by Major T J Atkinson and left centre, C Company by Captain C M Johnston. On the extreme left next to the

View of the positions of July 1. British trenches on the left, German trenches on the right. Note the field of fire of the German machine gun post in the foreground. This is on the approximate site of the Pope's Nose.

12/Royal Irish Rifles was D Company, commanded by Captain J G Brew. All companies were supported by Lewis gun crews.

The third wave of supporting attackers were accommodated in the communication trenches. It was intended that the attack be launched at 7.30am within 150 yards of the German front line. The distance between the two front lines was about 400 yards and so, at 7.10am, the first wave left the trenches followed by the second five minutes later.

Captain J G Brew.

The first wave got through the wire in front of the British positions easily enough, lines having been well cut previously, but by the time they reached the edge of the gully casualties were being taken from machine-gun fire, more especially enfilading from the high ground to the left. The second wave were under fire from the outset, this time from both flanks, including the higher ground from across the river where the Schwaben Redoubt was situated. During this time only one runner had got through with a single message. He had been sent by Captain Johnston of C Company when in a position still thirty yards short of the gully and asked for support. A supporting platoon was decimated when it went out. Soon after this Captain Johnston was killed. Most of the officers of C and D Companies had become casualties before the gully was reached and when in the comparative shelter of this position it was decided, because of the losses sustained, to amalgamate the two waves into one line. The advance continued but when within 150 yards of their objective came under further intense fire.

Meanwhile, the third and fourth waves had left their positions at 7.20am and 7.30am respectively but were caught in a severe artillery barrage which the Germans had put down between the British wire and the gully and they were practically annihilated by this together with the intense machine-gun fire before they got to the gully. Here, all the troops were impeded by large rolls of barbed wire thrown into it by the Germans.

The remains of the first and second waves launched themselves at the German front line and small groups of men got into the German trenches. The Germans, in places, held up their hands to surrender but soon realising how thinly numbered their attackers were, resumed the fight, especially as no support was forthcoming. Runners had been sent back but none survived to deliver their messages except Private Buckley who then collapsed and died from his wounds. The men of B

Dear M<u>rs</u> Mulholland,

Your husband L/Cpl J Mulholland 3361, 12 R.I.R has been officially reported as "missing" since the day the Ulster Division went into action. I write to offer you our deepest sympathy in your suspense and anxiety, and to express the hope that you may have heard of him from some reliable quarter, as it is to be feared that many of the "missing" have laid down their lives on the field of battle. Today there are many homes in Ulster where sorrow is and many hearts prostrate with grief. Ulster's sons fought a great fight and covered her name with glory. We are confident that you at home will meet these losses bravely and patiently, and will walk the hard path with unwavering faith, as those who have fallen would wish us to do. Let us comfort ourselves in the hope that beyond this world of sorrow and loss is God's world & He has gathered our own safely Home. Brave and courageous in life they are honoured among the fallen sons of the Empire and with their comrades they rest content - "until the day break and the shadows flee away".

I am, Yours in deep sympathy,

Andrew Gibson.

Lance Corporal S Mulholland, 12 Royal Irish Rifles, is commemorated on the Thiepval Memorial.

Company, commanded by Major Atkinson, appeared to have the greatest strength and a small body of men bravely penetrated the second and third German lines and were last reported near Beaucourt station.

We were to get to the station, Beaucourt sur Ancre station, and wait for the reserves to reach us. We got within a hundred yards of the station and I shot a German sentry.

We got into what must have been a German trench and waited for the rest but they never came. We could see Germans all around us. While we were in the trench before the station a sergeant asked us if we wanted to surrender. No surrender was

Rifleman F Kennedy, 12 Royal Irish Rifles, killed in action 1 July 1916. When Frank Kennedy was killed by a single bullet through the neck, his uncle Samuel Thompson *(right)* was at his side. When he saw that Frank was dead he took all his possesions, including his name tags and eventually returned them to his home in Armoy. There was, thus, no chance for an identified grave for Frank and he is commemorated on the Thiepval Memorial.

the shout alright. No surrender, no home rule, for God and Ulster! The sergeant went over to a young officer and they talked for a while. Then the officer waved a hand at us and shouted but we could not hear him. The 12 Rifles were down nearer the river and here the wire on the back side of the hill had not been cut except here and there. They were shot down as they tried to rush the Germans.

[Our scribe here is probably referring to the half of B company 12/Royal Irish Rifles who were allotted the task of covering the extreme right flank near William Redan. All other 12/Royal Irish Rifles should have been on his left]

At about 9.30am a mixed group of 9/Royal Irish Fusiliers and 12/Royal Irish Rifles gathered in the gully, where they discarded all surplus equipment and fought a retreat down to the road and the

Rifleman W J Morrow 12 Royal Irish Rifles aged twenty of Bushmills is commemorated on the Thiepval Memorial.

Rifleman R J Coleman 12 Royal Irish Rifles aged twenty one of Ballymaconnelly is commemorated on the Thiepval Memorial.

Rifleman John Murphy, 12 Royal Irish Rifles, aged twenty, of Ballymoney is buried in Knightsbridge British Cemetery.

Rifleman J Cochrane 12 Royal Irish Rifles aged twenty six of Bushmills is commemorated or the Thiepval Memorial.

railway line and back towards Hamel.

We were told that the Germans had taken back the front line we took less than an hour ago. We were ordered back. We dumped all our heavy stuff and made our way out over the railway lines to the river bank. Down by the bank we found some of the 12/Rifles. Some of the men who went back...made it to the ditch [gully] where they found men of the 12/Rifles. The Fusiliers and the Rifles put down a covering fire which helped some of us caught beyond the German front lines to make it down to the river bank and back to our own front lines. We put down covering fire and helped the men in the ditch get back as well. Only a quarter of us got back alive. We had to leave the young officer where he was because he was badly wounded and we could not take him with us.

As soon as the extent of the casualties was realised every man in the battalion was sent under the command of Major Pratt to hold the front line and two companies from the York and Lancs Regiment reinforced that position.

As already mentioned, the 9/Royal Irish Fusiliers were reinforced by half of B Company of the 12/Royal Irish Rifles. The idea was that they would be deployed on the right flank of the 12/Royal Irish Rifles and would attack an area of marshland on the right hand side of the railway line known as the Mound and a trench called Railway Sap which ran alongside the Hamel - Beaucourt road on the left hand side of the railway under a steep bank. It was known that Railway Sap contained many tunnel entrances which gave access to the German trench system running north towards Beaumont Hamel and probably linked up as far as Y Ravine.

It is not clear of what the Mound consisted. Certainly no raised natural feature would exist in the marshy ground of the Ancre valley and many trench maps appear to mistakenly position the Mound where there was actually a lake. It is likely that this was man-made and was either the remains of pre-war diggings by local people to create fishing lakes or was constructed by the Germans themselves as a strong point to defend the Hamel – Beaucourt road and the approach to Railway Sap, through which they fed their trench system.

At zero hour 12/Royal Irish Rifles Number 8 Platoon detailed to attack the position, led by

Rifleman J Black, Royal Irish Rifles of Ballymoney is commemorated on the Thiepval Memorial.

27

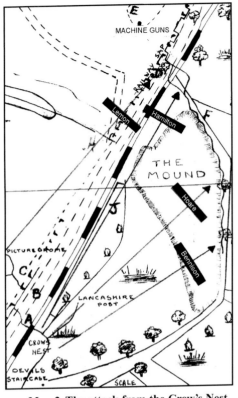

Map 2. The attack from the Crow's Nest.

Sergeant Hoare, left the Crow's Nest, an elevated piece of ground near the railway line, and advanced under a smoke barrage. They split into three groups:

Sergeant Bennison took a group to the right, Sergeant Hoare remained in the centre while Sergeant Hamilton went to the left. The shelling was very intense and all groups were heavily machine-gunned from both flanks. Sergeant Hoare's party soon all became casualties. On the left, Sergeant Hamilton also suffered heavily but managed to get three or four men into Railway Sap. On the right, Sergeant Bennison was killed and his party with its Lewis gun crew could not get forward at all. Sergeant Hamilton was driven out of the sap and Sergeant Hoare sent a runner back for orders to Colonel Blacker, the commanding officer. On receiving orders to retire he did so, with what was left of his men.

Number 6 Platoon was under the command of Lieutenant Lemon and left their position at the Picturedrome at the same time as the 9/Royal Irish Fusiliers on their left, before zero hour. However by the time they reached the gully, not more than fifty yards away, only Lieutenant Lemon and twelve men remained. There was no support, but Lieutenant Lemon advanced towards Railway Sap under cover of the high bank along the road. By the time he got to the German front

On the site of the German machine gun post that caught the Ulstermen so badly as they descended into the gulley. This is on top of the bank on the right of the entrance to the Ancre British Cemetery, where many of its victims lie.

line he only had nine men left. Lance Sergeant Millar and three men went to the left of the trench to bomb it from the bank above but were soon all hit. Lieutenant Lemon and the rest of the men got through the wire and advanced down Railway Sap but soon encountered thick wire protecting the entrance to a large tunnel. Rifleman Gamble, leading bayonet man, cut the wire, but there was a machine gun firing at them from a smaller tunnel further on down the trench. Lieutenant Lemon though, climbed the steep bank above, crawled along and bombed the position from above, allowing the men to pass. Just then, two German officers emerged from a dugout behind Lieutenant Lemon which connected to the tunnel and shot the British officer. Almost immediately, they themselves were dead, killed by a shell which landed in front of them. Lieutenant Lemon's remaining men were cut off between the German front and second lines and only two got away, Corporal Burgess and Rifleman McNeilly. Burgess got lost on the way back and McNeilly returned alone.

The two remaining platoons of B Company never left the British positions as they were held up by the 9/Royal Irish Fusiliers, whom they were following, although Captain C S Murray in command was wounded.

Later it was discovered that the two machine guns that caught Number 6 Platoon so badly were situated well forward of the German trench system in an elevated position, directly opposite the British line of advance and they had walked straight into them. These guns must also have inflicted many casualties on the ranks of all attacking battalions throughout that day and had not been silenced by Lieutenant Lemon and his remaining men, who, by keeping to the lower ground along the road, had missed them on the high bank on their left.

That evening parties all across the front went out into No Man's Land to try and locate the numerous wounded and bring them in. This activity continued the next morning on 2 July when, impelled by the grievous situation of their fellow men some went out in broad daylight to give assistance. One of these was Lieutenant Geoffrey St George Shillington Cather.

Consistently exposing himself to extreme danger, he was killed in the process and was subsequently awarded the Victoria Cross.

Lieutenant G St G S Cather VC.

I never really left the Hamel area. After the first few days we got a rest day and were set to work to dig communication trenches to the new positions and look for dead bodies and clear and rebuild our own trenches. The smell at times was awful. I got trench fever and was moved to hospital.

The desperate work continued until the morning of 5 July although the battalion was relieved on 2 July having suffered more than 86% casualties. All the officers were either killed, missing or wounded and out of approximately 600 that went into action 518 were similarly accounted for.

On 14 July the 9/Royal Irish Fusiliers Commanding Officer, Colonel Blacker, wrote to the Commanding Officer of the 10 Royal Irish Fusiliers, Colonel Fitzgerald, describing the recent events:

Dear Fitzgerald,

It is with a heavy heart I take up my pen to tell of the doings and losses of the battalion on July 1.

After being five days in the trenches during the preliminary bombardment, we came out for two days rest, then went on at midnight on June 30 and took up our positions ready for the assault which was for 7.30am July 1.

The battalion was on a full company front, each company being in a platoon front, thus being in four waves: two leading waves in the front trench line, third wave in the communication trench, fourth wave in the second line trenches. Order of companies A B C D. These dispositions were completed about 3.00am. We suffered fifty casualties while waiting. The opposing lines were about 400 yards apart with a ravine some 70 yards wide and steep banks about 20 feet high, about half way.

The order was for the leading wave to get within 150 yards of the German lines by 7.30am to be ready to assault the instant our barrage lifted at 7.30am. To do this the leading waves went over the parapet at 7.10am, 2nd waves at 7.15am, 3rd at 7.20am and the last waves at 7.30am.

Ensor, Atkinson, Johnston C, and Brew were in command respectively and 11 other platoon officers, that was all that were allowed in the actual assault: and about 600 men. Of these Johnston was killed. Atkinson, Townsend, Hollywood, Montgomery, Seggie, Stewart are missing, believed killed. Brew, Gibson Jackson, Shillington, Andrews, Smith, Barcroft, Capt Ensor are wounded and 518 other ranks are casualties.

57 killed
158 missing
303 wounded
Total 518

The 1st wave got away without suffering badly, the 2nd wave had many casualties, and the 3rd and 4th waves were mown down by machine gun fire, frontal and enfilade before they reached the ravine.

After the machine gun fire the Germans put a barrage between us and the ravine and few of C and D companies got to the German front line, but a number of A and B companies got through the German line and reached their objective at Beaucourt Station, past the German 3rd line. Of these none have returned. Owing to the failures of battalions on our left they were cut off.

The gallant and splendid leading of the officers and the steady advance of the men even after their officers were down, was magnificent, and makes me proud indeed to have been associated with such heroes.

For four nights after, parties went out and searched for the wounded and brought in several (Ensor and three others on the 4th night), and then we were moved back 12 miles and the Border Regiment continued the search and rescued many of which we owe them deep gratitude. Cather was killed bringing in wounded in daylight and Menaul slightly wounded. Alas, many of our best have gone and we only marched back 281 strong including transport.

The battalion in the hour of trial was splendid as I knew it would be, but I am heartbroken. The gallant friends and comrades we shall see no more. So few have come back unwounded it is hard to get any information as to individuals. Of the 48 Lewis Gunners, only 7 are left.

In 'A' Company, Sgts More, Whitsitt, Hegan, Kirkwood, McCourt are wounded and Sgt Wilson is missing believed killed. In 'B' Company, Sgt Porter is killed and Sgts Caulfield, Keith, Barr, Courtney, Johnston wounded. In 'C' Company, Sgts Hobbs and Bryans are killed and Sgts Brown, Love missing. In 'D' Company Sgts Mullen, Gorden, Thornberry killed, Sgts Hare, Balmer, Sewell, Hughes wounded and Sgt Bunting missing.

McClurg, the Primate's chauffeur, wounded. We want Lewis Gunners badly, the Signallers escaped well, we still have over 30 available. Your draft of 53 came last night and I saw them today, very well turned out and a good lot.

What can you do further? I fear little nearly all our bombing teams are gone. We are right back now, not more than 30 miles

Bringing in the wounded under fire.

31

from Boulogne and are hoping to get drafts and trying to refit and sort things out. Fortunately the four Company Sgt Majors and four Company Quarter Master Sgts were not allowed over the parapet so the Company Staff is intact.

Cather's loss is a severe one, he was quite wonderful as an Adjutant, but his was a glorious death and his name has gone in for a posthumous Victoria Cross. He brought in one wounded man from about 150 yards from the German wire in daylight! and was killed going out to a wounded man who feebly waved to him on his calling out to see if there were any more near.

There has been a lot of extravagant words written and published in the press, which is a great pity. The Division behaved magnificently and the point does not want labouring. Please be careful that this epistle does not get into the press.

I am still dazed at the blow and the prospect in front of us all but we must not be downcast; and must remember the glorious example of the gallant men who so nobly upheld the honour of the Battalion, and who have died so gloriously leaving their example to live after them and to inspire those who are left.

Much has already been written concerning the operation south of the river by the other half of the 108 Brigade and the 109 Brigade, of the 36th (Ulster) Division, who, in a determined and valiant effort got into the German lines and penetrated the Schwaben Redoubt. Mixed units of the 108 and 109 Brigades got through and past the left hand side of the Hansa Line and as far as Stuff Redoubt (*Fest Staufen*) on the right.

(See map 9 page 77 for locations)

The Schawben Redoubt (*Fest Schawben*) had been only lightly defended by units of a support company who were seemingly taken by surprise by the speed of the attack.

The German line south of the Ancre was defended by the 99 Reserve Infantry Regiment, part of the 52 Reserve Infantry Brigade, all Wurtemberg troops, belonging to the 26 Reserve Division. Their left battalion was defending Thiepval village, but their right battalion defending the Strasburg Line and Hansa Line was overrun, while the centre battalion at the redoubt was destroyed and over 500 prisoners were taken. The Ulstermen did not enter the depths of the redoubt, where, no doubt, many dangers lurked, but contented themselves with guarding the entrances and throwing in grenades and fire bombs. The Germans, further back in Grandcourt, could not determine whether the troops at the redoubt were friend or foe because of the dust and smoke.

The Ulstermen decided to push on and not wait until the appointed time of 10am and as a result got ahead of their own artillery barrage.

A German signaller attempts to get a message through.

Messages failed to get through.

Under desperate pressure, the 99/RIR repeatedly called for reinforcements. The Grandcourt Line was severely threatened while on the right there was fighting at the Stuff Redoubt. The German position was critical, the Ulstermen were only 100 yards from Grandcourt. General Von Soden, commanding the 26/Reserve Division, saw the redoubt as the key to events south of the Ancre, while his British counterparts considered Thiepval village more important. General Auwater, commanding the 52/RIB was ordered to retake the Schwaben Redoubt at all costs, and he sent a battalion of the 8/Bavarian RIR to reinforce it. At 11am, orders were issued for a counterattack which was to be a three pronged assault with units of the 52/RIB in the valley at St Pierre Divion on the German right. In the centre and on the left the remaining battalions of the 8 Bavarians would attack. In addition, machine gun companies were brought from across the river to the north, where the attack had been held.

It was 4pm before the attack was ready. Major Prager led three companies of the 180/RIR along the Ancre valley until they reached

The Germans counterattack.

Heinrich Trinkl, 1 Bavarian Regiment, from Munich. He was wounded and while in hospital in Brussels sent postcards written in mirror image in an attempt to maintain confidentiality. Photograph below shows wounded Germans in a Brussels hospital. (Trinkl third from right)

the Hansa Line, from where they bombed their way forward towards the redoubt. All the Ulstermen were either killed or taken prisoner. The centre attack derived from Stuff Redoubt and was led by Major Beyerholler and three companies of the 8/Bavarians. This was stopped by the British artillery. The left attack was made on the south-west corner of the redoubt by the remaining Bavarian units, but this was driven off. Meanwhile, Major Prager attacked the redoubt on the right, but he too, was driven back. Fresh attempts were made at 7pm but these also failed and both Major Prager and Major Beyerholler were casualties. Meanwhile, at 4.40pm the British 49th (West Riding) Division had been ordered to support the 36th (Ulster) Division. They had previously been in support to the attack on Thiepval village, where the British had concentrated their effort, and the Yorkshiremen were unable to reoganise and get forward until 8pm.

At 9pm all the guns in the 26th Reserve Division were ordered to turn on to the redoubt for one hour. At 10pm, the remaining German troops attacked again. For half an hour there was desperate hand to hand fighting after which the Ulstermen were overcome.

A German diarist described the situation as 'chaotic, strewn with over seven hundred dead of the gallant Ulster Division.'

The total casualties for the 36th (Ulster) Division on July 1 were 5,104.

The sight of so many of his friends killed and wounded on that day left a sorrow in his heart that stayed with him till the day he died. Now and then he would get up in the middle of the night when he could not sleep and light a candle and go down and make a drop of punch.

The Roll Call

Where an outcome has been found concerning any of the men mentioned in the narrative, it is given below.

Lieutenant W McCluggage is buried in Serre Road No 2 Cemetery
Lieutenant T G Haughton is buried at Hamel Military Cemetery
Sir Harry MacNaghten is commemorated on the Thiepval Memorial
Captain J Griffiths is buried in the Ancre British Cemetery
Major T J Atkinson is buried in the Ancre British Cemetery
Captain S Ensor survived his wounds
Captain C M Johnston is buried in Mesnil Communal Extension Cemetery
Private Buckley is recorded as killed in action in the battalion diary, but no trace of him has been found in the records of the Commonwealth War Graves Commision
Captain J G Brew survived his wounds, but was again wounded and died on a 6 April 1918 and is buried in Roye New British Cemetery
Sergeant Bennison, according to the battalion diary, was killed in action, but no trace of him can be found in the Commonwealth War Graves records
Lieutenant A D Lemon is commemorated on the Thiepval Memorial
Rifleman D J Gamble died of wounds 8 July 1916 aged 17. He was buried at Caudry Old Communal Cemetery, Nord
Captain C S Murray died of his wounds on 2 July 1916 and is buried in Warloy-Baillon Communal Cemetery Extension

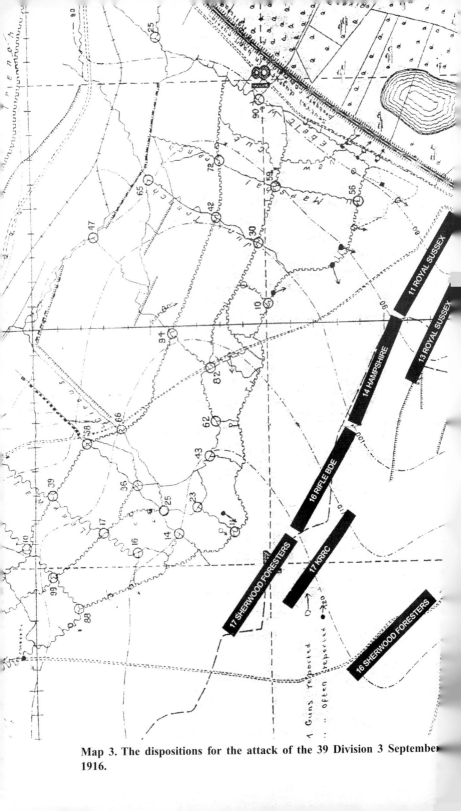

Map 3. The dispositions for the attack of the 39 Division 3 September 1916.

Chapter Two

SUNDAY 3 SEPTEMBER

The scenes in front of Hamel village were repeated nearly all along the sixteen mile front of the British offensive. Little was gained, except in the south, where the villages of Montauban and Mametz were captured, and, on 2 July, the village of Fricourt.

The British Army had suffered a grievous blow. On 3 July General Rawlinson held a meeting with the French General Foch. Things did not go well. Foch wanted the British to make further attacks on the Thiepval ridge and Pozieres, but Rawlinson objected, insisting that a further offensive, building on the gains further south would be more fruitful. As a result, Foch and General Joffre, the Supreme Commander of all Allied Forces in France, went to see Sir Douglas Haig at British Advanced GHQ. Haig reiterated the British position and re-affirmed that he did not have sufficient munitions and supplies for such an attack, although he had the manpower. (It would be interesting to know

Aerial view of the battlefield. July 1 attack by the Ulster Division started bottom right. September and November attacks from line of trees in cemetery and top of bank to the right. Cemetery lies in the Gully.

GERMAN FRONT LINE

for sure whether he was fully aware at that stage the extent of the British casualties). Joffre, however, would not budge and went as far as ordering the British Commander-in-Chief to make an attack. Haig demurred and stated his first priority and loyalty was to the British government and the meeting broke up.

39 Division

For these reasons, then, the Hamel-Beaucourt area became part of a 'quiet' sector. However, by September an offensive was proposed that would include Thiepval south of the River Ancre. This would be attacked by the 49th Division and the north bank of the Ancre, that is the same ground attacked by part of the 36th Division, just described, by the 39th Division.

After the attacks of 1 July the British realised that they needed to re-appraise the positions from which they had attacked and if possible increase the chances of the attacking troops actually getting into the enemy positions. At various points, therefore, the lines were straightened and pushed forward, where possible, to foreshorten the width of No Man's Land. The forward slopes of the 36th Division in front of Hamel had been horribly exposed and not only subject to frontal fire, but the failure of any attack on the flanks either in the direction of Beaumont Hamel on the left or Thiepval on the right, enabled any German machine guns in these sectors to turn their attentions in this direction and enfilade the attackers from both the left and the right.

The existence of the gully had been known, but its depth and the steepness of the sides, especially on the British side, badly underestimated and, in addition, the Germans had rolled masses of barbed wire into the bottom which was very difficult to negotiate. For these reasons the communication trenches were dug forward almost immediately after 1 July and the recovery of the dead and wounded was accompanied by the start of establishing new forward trenches mainly on the right and centre of the sector and these were to be known as Gordon Trench (front line) and Roberts Trench (second line). These were situated on the forward slope of the gully and linked up on the left under the embankment and with the sunken road near Mary Redan.

So the attack of the 3 September was, in theory, made from a more favourable position. However, in spite of Haig's assertion some two months earlier that manpower was not a problem, the 39th Division, especially the 116 Brigade on the right, was badly understrength. The 11/Royal Sussex could amass only 530 all ranks, the 12/Royal Sussex only 290 and the 13/Royal Sussex 375. The remaining battalion, the 14/Hampshire, had the most men at 570 all ranks.

The 116 Brigade occupied the right sector of the battle front, from the railway line on their right to their left where it joined 117 Brigade

38

sector was about 600 yards in length. The two front line battalions were the 11/Royal Sussex on the right and the 14/Hampshire on the left. Only the 13/Sussex was in support and there was no available reserve. In the valley by the railway and river, the 4/5/Black Watch were attached from the 118 Brigade to form a defensive flank and protect the right of the 11/Royal Sussex.

The formation in the 117 Brigade sector on the left consisted of 17/Sherwood Foresters (also known as the Welbeck Rangers) on the left and the 16/Rifle Brigade on the right. The 17/King's Royal Rifle Corps was in support and the 16/Sherwood Foresters (Chatsworth Rifles) in reserve. Prior to the attack, tunnels and saps had been driven forward. Roberts and Gordon Trenches, which overnight had been provided with solid duckboards, were very congested and many men chose to lie out in the comparative comfort of No Man's Land.

The attack was launched at 5.10am. On the extreme left, the 17/Sherwood Foresters (699 all ranks) had the furthest to travel and failed to reach the German front line before the British barrage lifted. An officer walking quickly across No Man's Land was still thirty yards short of the German trench with his laden men still a further fifty yards behind. This miscalculation was to be costly, as A and C Companies lost 50% of their men in No Man's Land while B Company reported 75%, all in about four minutes, the time they were given to get across. Major G Stollard, commanding A Company, got into the German front line at 6.00am and held on with Captain H V Walters, awaiting reinforcements which were sent at 7.15am, with two companies of the 17/King's Royal Rifle Corps going in. The situation was very confused and no messages were being received either by telephone or runners at battalion headquarters of the 17/King's Royal Rifle Corps. Lieutenant Spinney, a signals officer, decided to go forward by himself and find out what was happening. He crossed No Man's Land alone and jumped into the German front line trench and soon became involved in the

The British attack through a smoke screen. One man is already down.

close-quarter fighting taking place. He killed four Germans and eventually retraced his steps to battalion headquarters. Coming through the entrance, he was killed by a shell that landed nearby. The German second line was strongly held with machine guns and there was a desperate shortage of bombs. Further heavy casualties were taken and at 2.00pm a withdrawal was ordered. Back in Roberts Trench, under the shelter of the bank, Lieutenant Collen worked to reorganise what was left of the assaulting troops. There was no sign of Major Stollard or Captain Walters.

On the right of the 117 Brigade's sector the initial attack of the 16 Rifle Brigade failed to reach the German trenches but, supported by the 17/King's Royal Rifle Corps, they reached their first objective where they hung on (albeit not in the right position). The Germans counterattacked. They were in shirt sleeves carrying nothing except grenades and stick bombs and were easily able to outrange their attackers, who were short of bombs. Some men got into the second line, but were never seen again. The 16/Sherwood Foresters in reserve acted as carrying parties supplying the forward troops and some men crossed No Man's Land several times. Private Annable, having taken part in two raids, quickly carried messages and bombs and brought back a wounded man only to find that he was dead on arrival. He been shot again while on his back. Private Astle took charge of carrying parties following the loss of all the officers, making several journeys, keeping the men well disciplined and together. Private Armfeld bravely stayed alone at his forward post when all around him were dead and the position completely blown in.

On the right of the attack in 116 Brigade's sector, similar scenes occurred. On the left of the sector, the 14/Hampshire took heavy casualties from machine guns which seemed to be concentrated here, but some parties got into the German front line. The Germans were again standing up on the parapet of their trenches throwing grenades but the British machine guns soon shot them down. Second Lieutenant Leach led his men with great gallantry and gained a foothold in the German front line. Further advances were made towards the second and third line assisted by Captain Skinner and the Adjutant, Lieutenant Goldsmith, who had mustered all the men they could find. Captain Skinner was killed and Lieutenant Goldsmith wounded, but fought on, making blocks in the sections of captured trenches. The Hampshires hung on in the second line until 1.00pm where Second Lieutenant Tew was conspicuous in controlling his men's fire and killing many of the enemy himself. Lieutenant Ball and Lieutenant Bearn also did much

A group of King's Royal Rifle Corps men, probably 17 Battalion, taken early in 1916. Rifleman E A Jackson is at rear left.

Rifleman E A Jackson 17 King's Royal Rifle Corps, killed in action 3 September 1916, poses with his sisters, Eva (left) and Ida (right), with mother, Martha, seated.

good work, but later both these officers were killed. On retirement it was found that Lieutenant Tew and Lieutenant Bartlett were missing.

On the extreme right the 11 Sussex gained a foothold in the German second line. They were supported by 116 Brigade Machine Gun Corps who were already on their way forward at 5.00am, ten minutes before zero. No 1 Section did excellent work and eventually had three guns set up and working in the German second line. No 2 Section also made progress. One gun was blown up by a direct hit in the front line but two other guns were reported in the German third line with Lieutenant G R Greene. After the withdrawal at 2.00pm, No

1 Section remained in the German trenches and Sergeant Worthington, with Privates Humphries, Boulter and Neville were conspicuous in the action, only retiring at 7.10pm after fourteen hours in the German trenches. Nothing more was seen of or heard from Lieutenant Greene and No 2 Section, isolated deep in German territory.

A young officer in the 11/Royal Sussex later wrote of his experiences in the battle. Edmund Blunden was not in the front line attack, but gives an account of his part in his book *Undertones of War*. He was located, for the main part, in a position known as Kentish Caves, which is quite near the old British front line of 1 July.

So by 2.00pm it was all over and absolutely nothing had been achieved. The strength of the attack had been augmented when compared to that of 1 July, especially on the centre left and extreme left, where only three companies had operated in the earlier battle. On the right, although three battalions had been used, all were understrength.

Edmund Blunden

It is quite clear from the accounts given that an acute shortage of bombs (hand grenades) contributed to the failure of the attack. The men were equipped with large quantities of SAA (small arms ammunition) which was largely unused and mostly abandoned, but carried only two Mills bombs each, with instructions to stockpile them. However, with so many casualties in No Man's Land the bombs never arrived in sufficient numbers and those that did were mainly used by individual soldiers to defend themselves.

The casualties of the 39th Division for 3 September were:-

	Killed	Wounded	Missing		
Officers	36	59	32		
Other Ranks	234	1558	899		
	270	1617	931	=	2,818

South of the river the attack was undertaken by the 49th (West Riding) Division. The 146 Brigade was nearest the river with the 1/6/West Yorkshire and the 1/8/West Yorkshire battalions leading the assault. The 147 Brigade were on their right and here the 1/4/Duke of Wellington's and the 1/5/Duke of Wellington's were in front. After the barrage the troops moved across No Man's Land and some of the German front line positions were taken. However the 1/5/Dukes lost some direction and veered to the right and missed a fortified salient on their right known as

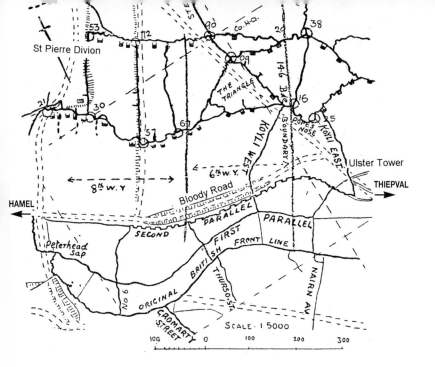

Map 4. Attack, 3 September, 1916, 49 Division south of the Ancre.

the Pope's Nose. Although the attack had been supported by a massive gas and ammonal bomb attack, the Germans managed to stage a strong counterattack and this was supported by strong machine-gun fire from the Schwaben Redoubt and the Strasburg Line.

Down the slope towards the valley, the units of the West Yorks were caught by this fire and also from the fire from the Pope's Nose in the front line. Many were struck down in No Man's Land and some of those retreating took refuge in the Thiepval – Hamel road, only to be shelled. Scenes there were similar to those of 1 July. Early morning mist had prevented visual signalling and the situation was unclear for some time. The attack had commenced at 5.13am but, by 7.00am, men started to drift back, and by 7.30am all the West Yorks who could make it were back. The Duke of Wellington's men hung on until all their officers were either killed or wounded and ammunition had nearly run out. By 10.00am those that were able to do so had also returned to the sanctuary of their own trenches.

The attack seems to have had little chance of success and the inexperienced men had been very tired from the outset. Nevertheless, High Command later criticised the men for apathy and lack of determination.

... recruities on 3 September 1916.

The Roll Call.

Major G Stollard is commemorated on the Thiepval Memorial

Captain H V Walters is buried in the Ancre British cemetery

Lieutenant K T Spinney is buried in Knightsbridge Cemetery

Private W Annable was killed in action 17 June 1917, and is buried in Hop Store Cemetery, Ypres

Private H Astle was wounded in July 1917, evacuated to England, but died and is buried in Ford Park Cemetery, Plymouth

Private Armfeld survived the war

Lieutenant T S Leach was awarded the Military Cross

Lieutenant F B Goldsmith was promoted to Major, won the MC and Bar, was killed in action on 27 September 1917 and is commemorated on Tyne Cot Memorial, Belgium

Captain F T Skinner is buried in Serre Road No1 Cemetery

Second Lieutenant Tew was captured and became a prisoner of war

Second Lieutenant B H Ball is commemorated on the Thiepval Memorial

Second Lieutenant P D Bearn is commemorated on the Thiepval Memorial

Second Lieutenant E F P Bartlett was wounded upon retiring and fell into a shell hole, where he remained for two days, before crawling back to the British front line

Lieutenant G R Greene is commemorated on the Thiepval Memorial

Sergeant J Worthington died of wounds on 4 September 1916 and is buried in Acheux British Cemetery

Lieutenant E Blunden was awarded the Military Cross in November 1916 and survived the war, becoming a writer and Professor of English

Private J Turnbull is buried in Connaught Military Cemetry

Private John Turnbull, Duke of Wellington's Regiment. Son of a Yorkshire Dales farmer, keen to enlist, typical of those accused of apathy. Killed in action 3 September 1916.

RECALLING THOSE PROUD FEATS OF "PORTSMOUTH'S OWN" HEROES

SEPTEMBER is a proud month of memories of undying glory earned for Portsmouth, themselves, and posterity by volunteer troops from the City and environs who, with caps and cigarettes at jaunty angles, assaulted Beaumont Hamel and Flers at appalling cost during the Somme battles of World War I.

...ty-one years ago on Sunday, ...and 3rd "Portsmouth's Battalions (later to become ...h, 15th, and 16th Hampshire Regiment) were formed in when the Kaiser's troops ...arving through all fronts, ...r honour of being the first ...r Flers.

...s had been used for the ...me, and German gunnery's who had "formed-fours" ...outhsea Common and ...r proudly behind their ...rough Portsmouth's defied 50yd. belts of wire ...ky traps to gain their

...etion for this went to the ...ttalion. They went in ...strong, and at roll-call ...vs later, about 173 names

...following month, ...al H. Rawlinson, com-ng the 4th Army, "To assault presented by the of strongly-defended systems and capture ...lage of Flers as well, rush, was a feat of ...f which every officer, ...and man may feel proud."

OO, am one of the 14th ...ants survivors, having been ...usly wounded in that ...e.

'e went over the top at 5.10 morning. Being in "A" pany I was in the first ...e, but very few reached the ...man line.

'e were told that there were ...g conscripts facing us with ...ew old sweats to stiffen ...n, but what a surprise we

'he enemy threw everything ...us. The idea was to attack ...keep the enemy occupied, ...le right and left were to be ...ced back causing the Ger-ns to retire to straighten the

shall always remember the ...rage shown by our stretcher ...rers.

...f any of the boys left ...hall be glad to see them.

W. E. V. Dicks.

Sunday, September 15, is this year the date coinciding with ...ortsmouth's added pride in sharing in Britain's commemorative tribute to Battle of Britain pilots of World War II.

Therefore, Sunday's Battle of Britain parade by the Portsmouth branch of the Royal Air Forces Association to St Mary's Church, Kingston, will hold an even more personal interest for members of the flourishing "Portsmouth's Own" Battalions Old Comrades Association (1914-18).

Following the example of recent years, they have decided again to follow the ex-R.A.F. men on parade, headed by their two standards presented by the Portsmouth public by subscription and which were saved from the blitz on the City.

The veterans will also march with memories of the 1st "Ports-

...mouth's Own" 14th Service Battalion. The Hampshire Regiment which, at 5.55 a.m. on September 3, 1916, went over the top at Beaumont Hamel, fully aware of the immensity of the task.

After the action, when roll-call was taken, out of 1,200 personnel, only one officer and 90 men were there to answer.

The battalion was under the command of Major Skinner, master at Portsmouth Grammar School.

The only officer who survived the Beaumont Hamel attack was Lieut. Goldsmith, who won the distinction of becoming the youngest serving lieutenant colonel. He was later killed in action.

PROUD NAME

At "Portsmouth's Own" Association's September meeting, the Secretary, Mr. R. White, expressed regret that "a lot of people forget us" despite the Battalions' proud name in the City and district.

"We want to remind them," he said, urging a strong muster of members on Sunday.

Tomorrow, members of the Association are having an evening outing to Swanwick for supper, and on return will attend a dance at the Dockyard Club.—W.D.H.C.

Pte W E V Dicks, 14 Hampshire, wounded on 3 September but survived to remember.

Conversation of 2nd. Lt. Bartlett, 14th. Bn. Hamp. R.

taken down by Major Lytton at No. C.C.S. GEZAINCOURT, Sept.6th.1916

Narrative of what happened during the attack on enemy trenches N.

of the river ANCRE on September 3rd. 1916

I was on the extreme left of the Hants attack. I was supposed to go over with the 3rd. wave; but there was confusion at once and the waves immediately got intermingled. Probably we followed our own barrage up a little too closely. I remember coming under M.G. fire immediately we left our own trenches. When I reached the enemy parapet I was hit by shrapnel in the head and for the moment I was stunned and lost consciousness. On coming to, our men were holding the enemy front line. I became unconscious again, and when I again came round the enemy was bombing us from both flanks. We tried to block the trench on either flank and also the communication trenches, - as shown below -

We had two Lewis Guns besides a certain amount of our own and German bombs. Our right flank was secure, but the left flank a bit shaky. We successfully held off the enemy attacks as long as our bombs lasted, and then we went on fighting with L.Gs and rapid fir 2/Lt. Tew fought magnificently, he controlled the fire and used the bombs with the utmost discretion. Furthermore, he shot many of the enemy himself. Also 2nd. Lts. Burn and Ball of the Hants and 2nd. Lt. Tennant of the Rifle Brigade did very well, also a Hants Sergeant and a Sussex Corporal - names unknown.
Finally when our ammunition ran out, the order was given to retire, and then it was a case of "sauve qui peut". If we had had about 100 more bombs we could have hung on indefinitely.
I was sniped just as I got through the German wire, and was hit in the shoulder, I fell into a crump hole and made myself as comfortable as possible. Private Diver of the Hants bound me up, and acted with great courage. I lay there till dusk when another wounded man of the Hants crawled in. I had my ground sheet and an air pillow. It was impossible to get out of the hole at night as the M.G. fire was too intense. About 4 a.m. the morning of the 4th. I tried to crawl out, but was again sniped - shot through the same shoulder. I got into another crump hole near by and waited with this man all day. At night I again crawled out and succeeded in reaching our parapet without being hit. I believe my companion was again hit on the way back, but I sent the stretcher bearers of the Cheshires after him and they brought him in.
On reaching our lines, I found Padre Thom of the Hants acting with great gallantry bringing in wounded men under fire. The Cheshire stretcher bearers were also magnificient.

ENEMY TRENCHES

The enemy trenches were Splendid ~~magnificent~~, much deeper than ours - well revetted with timber - a strong wooden fire step, Good dug-outs under the parapet with steps running down - Practically one to each bay - There were a few enemy dead in the bays, probably all that were in the front line which was very lightly held.

/3. IDENTIFICATION.

Second Lieutenant Bartlett returned after being missing for two days to make this report.

63 (ROYAL NAVAL) DIVISION

The division was principally made up of men from the various Naval Reserve formations for whom, in August 1914, no place could be found on a ship. By 1916 these men formed two of the brigades in the division, while the third was made up of conventional army infantry battalions

63th (Royal Naval) Division

188 Brigade
Anson Battalion
Howe Battalion
1/Royal Marine Battalion
2/Royal Marine Battalion

189 Brigade
Hood Battalion
Nelson Battalion
Hawke Battalion
Drake Battalion

190 Brigade
1/Honourable Artillery Company
7/Royal Fusiliers
4/Bedfordshire
10/Royal Dublin Fusiliers

Royal Naval Division Silk Postcard.

A detailed account of their origins can be found in Douglas Jerrold's *The Royal Naval Division* or *The Hawke Battalion*, for example, but they were a very mixed lot of men who included retired marine sergeants and fishermen from the Hebrides who bonded into an enthusiastic brotherhood of amateur soldiers. They seemed to develop their own way of doing things, ignoring some of the more traditional army dogma in favour of more realistic arrangements. All this was fine until their commanding officer, seemingly 'loved' by all, Major General Sir Archibald Paris was wounded while making a reconnaissance of the trenches prior to the November attack and had to be replaced.

His successor, Major General

Major General Sir Archibald Paris.

47

C D Shute, was a traditional army man and soon felt the need to make some changes. At one stage he proposed that some of the RND officers should be replaced by army officers, but this was resisted. For some amusing detail of this I again refer the reader to Jerrold's book, suffice to reprint here the words of a ditty written by A P Herbert and sung to a popular tune of the day.

The General inspecting the forces
Exclaimed with a terrified shout
I refuse to command a division
That leaves its excreta about

But nobody took any notice
No one was prepared to refute
That the presence of shit was congenial
Compared to the presence of Shute

And certain responsible critics
Made haste to reply to his words
Observing that his staff advisers
Consisted entirely of turds

For shit may be shot at odd corners
And paper supplied there to suit
But a shit would be shot without mourners
If someone shot that shit Shute

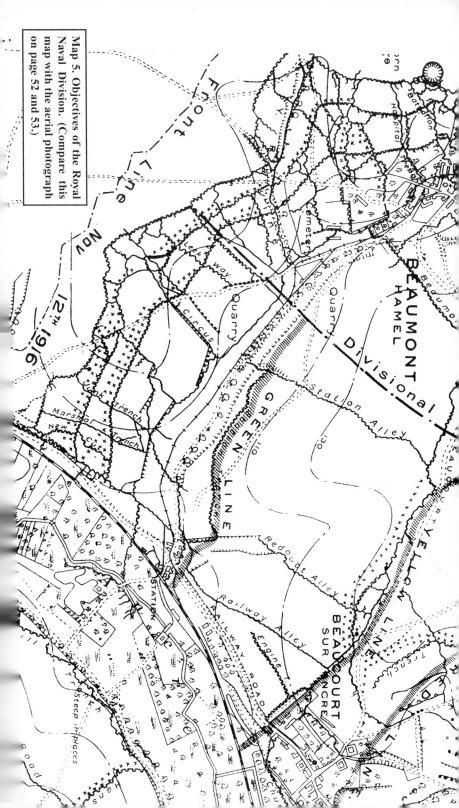

Map 5. Objectives of the Royal Naval Division. (Compare this map with the aerial photograph on page 52 and 53.)

Chapter Three

MONDAY 13 NOVEMBER

The attack as planned was different to many others in that the initial battalions were to have quite short range objectives where, once achieved, the attackers would wait and then be overtaken or 'passed over' by a supporting battalion. Much detailed planning and organisation had taken place and the original date of the attack, 23 September, postponed several times owing to the weather. There had been a lot of rain.

It will be recalled that the almost lightweight attack of 3 September

Winter in the Ancre Valley, 1916.

consisted of just eight battalions, most of which were understrength. By contrast, for the attack of 13 November, the full weight of the 63th Division was thrown against the German positions. This consisted of two brigades of Naval personnel, making eight battalions, and a further brigade of conventional infantry making twelve in all. Add to this the four battalions of the 111 Brigade belonging to the 37th Division who were brought in to the battle on 14 November, and it can be seen that General Gough, commanding Fifth Army, did not intend to allow the operation to fail for lack of weight. However, once again, many of the battalions were understrength.

Sir Douglas Haig was concerned to avoid an assault in unfavourable conditions and on 12 November went to see General Gough at Fifth Army Headquarters. The preliminary bombardment had already begun. Haig said that success was much needed as it would have valuable repercussions on the Eastern Front, but he did not want to take risks. Gough reassured him that the break in the weather would provide

the opportunity to attack which, if not taken then, would result in him having to withdraw his troops, as they had been subjected to adverse conditions for too long waiting to attack. Many of the battalions were now understrength owing to illness. Haig was reassured and agreed that the attack should go ahead.

Aerial view of the right and centre section of the German front.

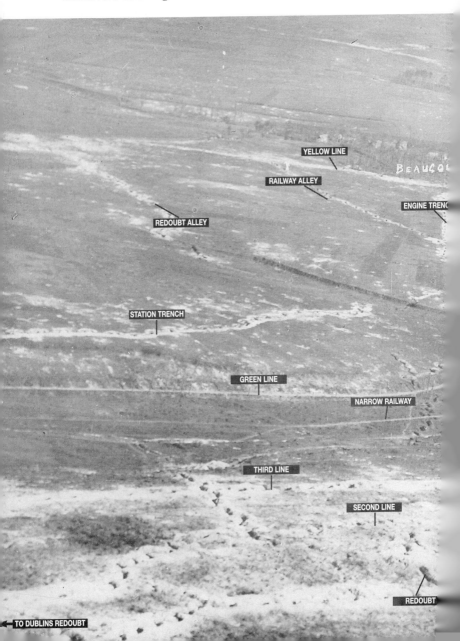

The frontage of the attack was about 1,200 yards, each battalion front about 300 yards and it had the support of brigade machine gun companies and light trench mortar batteries. There were three main objectives. The Green Line, which was a trench called Station Trench, was situated on top of the bank on the right hand side of the road between Beaucourt Station and Beaumont-Hamel. The Yellow Line was a trench that ran along the left hand side of the road from

The German second and third line trenches as denoted by the chalk marks on the right show up well. Similiar but less well defined disturbance to the immediate right of the Cemetery marks the British front line.

Beaucourt sur l'Ancre to Beaumont-Hamel. The final objective was the Red Line which was to be established beyond the environs of Beaucourt sur l'Ancre.

There were intermediate objectives, such as the Dotted Green Line which was the German third line trenches, but in the interest of simplicity we will deal only with the main objectives. As mentioned, the idea was that the attacking battalions would reach their objectives, consolidate and await the arrival of the supporting battalion who would then pass through to the next objective.

Map 6. Original map showing state of the road from Hamel to German front line.

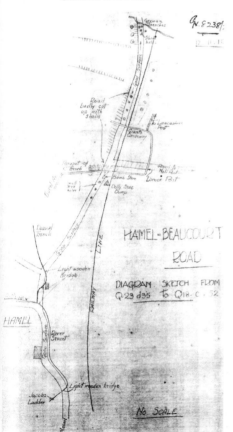

Overnight the sky cleared, but the resulting drop in temperature caused the damp ground to throw up a thick mist. It was still dark at 5.45am when the attack went in on a four battalion frontage. Whether the thick mist that prevailed was more of an advantage to the attacking force than a disadvantage to the defenders is difficult to decide. Certainly the Germans were surprised and could not see their attackers but neither could the British see where they were going and direction was quickly lost. In certain places in the German lines, the effect of the barrage and the swamp like conditions had reduced

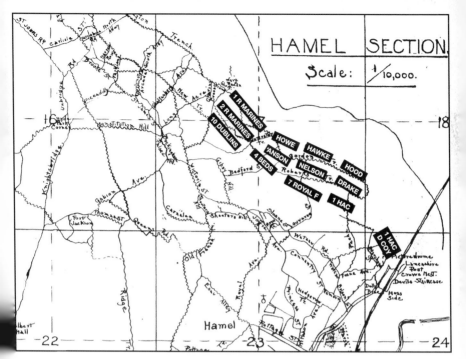

Map 7. Dispositions of the Royal Naval Division, 13 November, 1916.

the trenches to little more than a depression and men passed over these positions without realising it. Furthermore, many dugouts were missed and the occupants were able to inflict heavy casualties on the supporting battalions.

To deal more specifically with the attack let us start with the battalions on the extreme left where, it will be recalled, the divisional boundary was at Mary Redan. It will be seen from the map (above) that the 1/Royal Marines and the Howe Battalion were in front, supported

Germans troops await an attack.

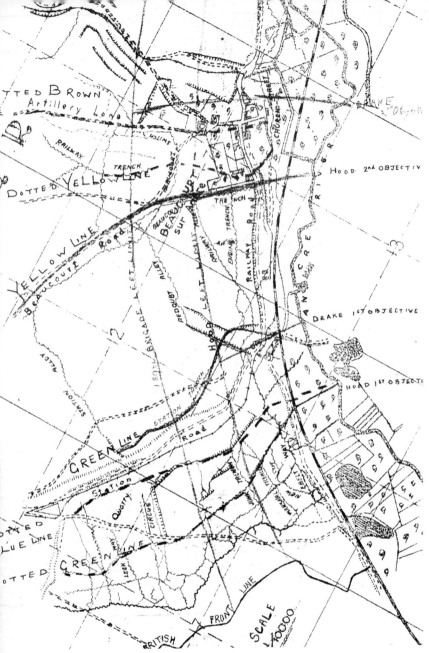

Map 8. Original map used by 189 Brigade.

by the 2 Royal Marines and the Ansons. The 1 Royal Marines were commanded by Lieutenant Colonel F J W Cartwright and took half of their casualties for the whole battle in the first few minutes crossing

No Man's Land, when every company commander was killed and comparatively few men reached the enemy front line. This was mainly owing to shellfire which was very heavy as they dragged themselves through the clinging mud, which impeded their progress. Some men somehow made it through to the German second line, and then the third line, where they were engaged in hand-to-hand combat.

Their sister battalion fared little better. The Commanding Officer, Lieutenant Colonel A R H Hutchinson, went over waving his cap and shouting, 'Come on Royal Marines!' and an attempt was made to dribble a football across No Man's Land. Some of their number also got into the German third line and were involved in heavy hand-to-hand fighting, but were either killed or pushed back. The 7/Gordon Highlanders of the 51st (Highland) Division on their left had fallen back, which left that flank exposed. Nevertheless, a mixed detachment of marines was reported to be fighting later with the 51st Division, west of Station Road near Beaumont Hamel.

Almost everything had been hit by shells and it was one continual mass of debris and mud pools. Some were half filled with water and many had wounded men lying helpless in them – ghastly sights. The German trench we were in was in a chronic state. Once you took a step you had a job to get your leg out, the mud being so deep and sticky. Wounded Germans and our men were lying all over the place. What had been dugouts were now partly closed by the muddy landslides that had taken place...and choked the entrances.

Remains of the railway along the Ancre Valley.

The adjutants of both battalions were casualties in the German second line. Captain C G Farquharson (2/Royal Marines) was wounded and Captain C L Muntz, (1/Royal Marines) was mortally wounded.

On their right, Howe also advanced in irregular formation, rather bunched up, to be followed by the Ansons and then the 4/Bedfords. No reports came back and nothing could be seen, but tremendous machine-gun fire was heard especially from the left and fierce bombing activity on the right. Eventually, Signal Officer Sub Lieutenant Fletcher decided to go forward to see what was happening but was immediately shot as he got onto the German parapet. Howe, with their right flank dangerously exposed, fought hard to reach the German third line, but were hit by both frontal and enfilade fire from the right. They lost every company commander in the process. Lieutenant A F Maynard and Lieutenant C D F De la Mothe, leading the first companies across, were both killed having penetrated through to the third line and later Lieutenant Commander Edwards was wounded. Lieutenant Sprange and about twenty men eventually held on in the third line where Sprange, too, was wounded but he refused to be taken back and stayed to direct his men. At 7.30am Howe established

Second Lieutena **C W Martin, Ro** **Marines, aged** **nineteen. A** **promising actor** **his time, he had** **trained at RAD** **and apeared at t** **Savoy Theatre** **under the direct** **of Henry Irving** **also appeared a** **the Haymarket** **Royalty Theatre** **He is buried in** **Ancre British** **Cemetery.**

58

Station Road (Green Line) to where Lieutenant Commander Gilliland broke through.

headquarters in the German lines and took over a dugout from some Germans who were sheltering in it. The seventeen Germans were put to work straight away carrying back the wounded.

The Ansons, who had already lost their commanding officer, Lieutenant Colonel F J Saunders, killed before the attack by shellfire, were led by Lieutenant Commander J M Gilliland. They suffered many casualties in No Man's Land. The German lines on the right held out, but on the left Commander Gilliland broke through with some men of the Anson, Howe and Nelson and advanced towards Station Trench (Green Line).

Lieutenant Commander Gilliland wrote:

The composite party I had numbered about ninety and consisted mainly of Ansons with some Howes and Nelsons and later a few Gordon Highlanders. The Howe battalion should have advanced through us to the second objective, the Yellow Line, but by the time the barrage lifted the Howes had not arrived, being held up with the Ansons in the enemy front line system. I therefore advanced to the Yellow Line. On the way we suffered considerable casualties from machine-gun fire from our right front and the enemy put down a heavy barrage on the Yellow Line.

...tenant L M
...es Royal
...rines, aged
...teen. Killed
...ction 13
...ember 1916,
... buried in
...ly Wood
...etery.

Lieutenant L J A Dewar, Royal Marines, aged twenty. Killed in action 13 November 1916 and is buried in the Ancre British Cemetery.

DEWAR.—To the beloved memory of my darling sons, DAVID (SONNIE), Lt., M.G.C., B.A., LL.B. Camb., mentioned in dispatches, aged 24 ; JACK, 2nd Lt., R.M.L.I., aged 20, both killed in France ; and of their dear Father, DAVID DEWAR, M.A., Vicar of Holy Trinity, Loughborough, who died 5th Aug., 1921, aged 59.

We were entirely isolated and enfiladed from the right. Efforts to get in touch with troops on the flanks were unsuccessful. Messages were sent to Headquarters but failed to get through.
Lieutenant Commander Gilliland returned to Station Road, (Green Line). Surgeon C H Gow was badly wounded but refused to give up; his last task had been to write a report about the heroism of the stretcher bearers before he died. It was decided to attempt to reorganise and make an advance from the German second line on Station Road (Green Line) at 9.30am and then on to Beaucourt Road (Yellow Line), where it had been reported that two battalions were holding out. Lieutenant Colonel Cartwright, assisted by Lieutenant Colonel Hutchinson, assembled a mixed force of about 100 men, under the command of Captain Gowney, comprising men of the Royal Marine battalions, Anson and Howe. They were held up by machine-gun fire from a strongpoint on their right and built a block for

Sub Lieutenant E M Aron 189 Brigade Machine Gun Company Royal Naval Division – killed in action 13 November. Pictured while at Jesus College Cambridge.

protection in the trench that led in that direction. There was exceptionally heavy machine-gun fire from the third line, as well, and the advance was checked. A request for artillery support only resulted in the ensuing barrage falling on themselves and a number of casualties occurred before the mistake could be rectified. The assault succeeded in reaching the enemy third line but it soon became clear that the Germans still held most of this position, as well as parts of the second line; and the front line had not been properly cleared either. Two hours later, just two men, Lieutenant Commander B H Ellis and one other rank, arrived in Station Road, where they found Lieutenant Commander Gilliland with about 200 men.

Co-ordinated with this attempt to get to Station Road, a bombing attack on the right at 9.30am was led by Commander W G Ramsay-Fairfax, commanding officer of the Howe Battalion, and the enemy was driven back. A dugout was captured with twenty Germans and they released two wounded prisoners, but the attack could not be sustained as the German bombers were able to out-throw their assailants with grenades and stick bombs. A 'stop' was then built across the trench to consolidate the ground won. At about 3.00pm, the Howe again attempted to push forward into the German third line and establish battalion

Dead British machine gunners.

headquarters, but resistance was too strong. Here, Lieutenant Sewell, Royal Field Artillery Forward Observation Officer, was killed and Lieutenant Aston, Lewis Gun Officer, was also shot dead by a sniper.

At 11.55am, Lieutenant Commander Gilliland advanced again towards Beaucourt Road (Yellow Line), leaving battalion headquarters in Station Road with six men. By 12.45pm nothing further had been heard of Gilliland, and Lieutenant Commander Ellis led a party forward to reconnoitre. The patrol observed the southern part of the Yellow Line held by troops, but with their left flank completely exposed and with the enemy in force at that point, coming under fire, they returned to Station Road. At dusk the Anson Battalion Headquarters retired to the German third line and joined with the headquarters of the 1/Royal Marines and 2/Royal Marines. During the night of 13/14 November, Station Road was occupied under cover of darkness. At 4.00am on the 14 November, the Ansons, led by Captain Gowney their adjutant, with details of 1/Royal Marines, 2/Royal Marines, 10/Dublins and 4/Bedfords advanced to the Green Line where they made contact with the 7/Gordon Highlanders of 51st Division on the left of Station Alley. Their right flank towards Beaucourt Station, however, was unprotected. Here they dug in, the only officers present were Lieutenant Commander Ellis and Captain Gowney, (Anson), Lieutenant van Praagh, (1/Royal Marines) Surgeon McBean-Ross, (2/Royal Marines), Lieutenant Colonel Cartwright, and Lieutenant Colonel Hutchinson, who then took command of the operations in Station Road for the next two days.

We can now turn to the initial attack on the right. From the map it will be seen that the Hawke and Hood battalion were in the front line, followed by Nelson and Drake, with 1 Honourable Artillery Company and 7/Royal Fusiliers in support.

The Hawke Battalion were just right of the centre of the attack and, as such, it transpired, were opposite a large redoubt cleverly disguised. Nobody knew it was there. It had many entrances at the front, sides and rear, all bristling with machine guns, and commanded a field of fire over most of the battlefield. A single burst of fire hit Lieutenant Colonel L O Wilson, commanding the Hawke Battalion, Lieutenant Bowerman, together with Lieutenant Edwards, the signalling officer, and Petty Officer McDonald who both got up and attempted to continue but were immediately shot down again and killed. Indeed the whole battalion suffered grievous losses and three company commanders fell too. In the words of the diarist, 'The Hawke Battalion after the first few minutes of the attack no longer existed as a unit'. Some men managed to scramble forward and pass either side of the redoubt and eventually joined up with Lieutenant Colonel Freyburg, commanding the Hood Battalion. Attempts were made to pass the redoubt on either side. One of these was led by Lieutenant The Honourable Vere Harmsworth with a part of B company who succeeded in getting past the left of the redoubt and into the second line, although Harmsworth was wounded. He was wounded again attempting to get forward and did not survive. Lieutenant D Jerrold all but had his arm severed.

Lieutenant Col
L O Wilson
commanding
Hawke Battal

Surgeon J S V

Lieutenant The Hon.
V S T Harmsworth.

Men of The Royal Naval Division, possibly Hawke Battalion, Joseph Elliott is on the extreme left.

After Petty Officer Joseph Elliott, (Hawke) was killed only his personal effects were found, in the back of a German dugout. Was he taken prisoner or perhaps a medic took them from him? Among these were his New Testament and a Turkish watch which must have been obtained in Gallipoli. The inscription on the inside cover is very clear.

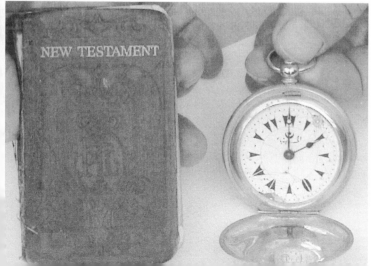

Surgeon J S Ward went forward with Surgeon Cox of the Nelson Battalion, but Doctor Ward was killed by a grenade that was thrown at him. Later in the day, Major Norris and Sub Lieutenant A P Herbert went forward but apart from a few small groups of men could find no trace of the battalion. A short time later, Major Norris was shot through the chest by a sniper.

Those men from Hawke who did get through did so mainly by passing the redoubt widely to the right where the ground sloped away and was 'dead' to the German machine gunners. Here, Sub Lieutenant Stewart and Sub Lieutenant Henderson got through with about eighteen men, together with some of the Hood Battalion. Stewart had taken a Lewis gun with him and did some good work in Station Road (Green Line) before reaching the area around Beaucourt Station, where both officers were wounded. Thus these short paragraphs tell the essential story of the Hawke Battalion. Every officer was a casualty and the number of men who returned unscathed amounted to about twenty. Prior to the battle, the battalion had lost about 150 men owing to sickness because of the poor conditions and had gone into the attack about 460 strong. The casualty rate was over 95%.

The Nelson Battalion followed Hawke into the attack but, although supposed to be only 150 yards behind the last wave of Hawke, could see nothing, only the reflection of the flash of the artillery shells on their bayonets in the darkness. The first two waves met frontal machine-gun fire, but some of their number managed to get into the German front line and through towards the second line. The second and third waves, though, encountered very intense enfilading fire and suffered very heavy casualties, losing both cohesion and direction and except for just a few isolated groups, ceased to exist as a fighting force. At 6.30am the Nelson Battalion had attempted to move their headquarters forward from the gully just behind Roberts Trench. They could not have chosen a worse location and in the fog walked straight into the machine gun emplacements at the redoubt. They were hit at close range and many were killed, including Lieutenant Colonel N O Burge, the commanding officer and the Adjutant, Sub Lieutenant J H Emerson.

Lance Corpor
F E Gee, killed
action 13
November 191
from Sittingbo
Buried in the
British Cemet
His headstone
his age as
seventeen, but
was twenty or
sister, aged or
nine, died of
diptheria just
before he was
killed.

Lieutenant Colonel N O Burge commanding the Nelson Battalion.

64

Sub Lieutenant G Reddick, aged twenty two, Nelson Battalion, killed in action 13 November 1916.

With all the officers casualties, Petty Officer Wilson rallied all the men he could find but eventually they too were all casualties.

About 100 of the Nelson men had got through to the Green Line (Station Trench) and were isolated, inititially failing to get in touch with Commander Gilliland. At the lifting of the barrage, they duly followed their orders and continued to advance towards the Beaucourt Road (Yellow Line), where they found no one else and both of their flanks exposed. Later a message got through that other troops, led by Lieutenant Commander Gilliland, were holding the same line further east towards Beaucourt village and they moved in that direction until contact was made. The writer of the Nelson's diary recorded the familiar words, 'At this point the Battalion ceased to exist as an identity'.

On the extreme right of the attack Hood led the way, followed by Drake. On the right of Hood, a company of the 1/Honourable Artillery Company was attached with special responsibility for the railway line and the area around the Mound near the river bank. They had also to clear the dugouts and tunnels in the high bank along the Hamel-Beaucourt road.

Lieutenant Colonel Freyberg DSO VC.

Hood was commanded by Lieutenant Colonel B C Freyberg and the company commanders were Lieutenant F S Kelly, Captain The Hon S L Montague, Lieutenant S H Fish and Sub Lieutenant C F Callingham. Other ranks numbered about 535. The barrage which opened at zero hour had also done so at that time for several days previously, in an attempt to lull the Germans into believing this was just a ploy and that the attack would come at some other time and place. The objective of the Hood was the German third line where they would be leap frogged by Drake but, because of the darkness and the difficulty in recognising any of the German positions, the waves and companies became mixed up.

Under strict instructions to keep up with the barrage, the men pushed on, especially on the right, and passed their objective and found themselves near Beaucourt Station at about 6.15am. Later, two companies of the Drake Battalion also arrived as well as some of 1 Honourable Artillery Company and a battle for the station ensued as daylight came. Eventually, the station was captured and over 400 prisoners were taken in dugouts situated in Station Road. The outskirts

Beaucourt-Hamel station.

of Beaucourt (Yellow Line) were reached, but the men had to fall back as they were caught in their own barrage

The Hood troops, more to the left, however, encountered resistance in the German front line. Lieutenant Fish and Sub Lieutenant Callingham were wounded here but the battle was carried successfully to the third line, where Lieutenant Kelly led a successful attack on a bombing post, but he was killed. Fighting was intense, many prisoners were taken, but casualties were also heavy. Further forward with Lieutenant Colonel Freyberg, casualties were also caused by the heavy artillery firing short, although the eighteen pounders were mostly accurate. Men had to be brought back twice to avoid their own guns and were still being prevented from occupying the Yellow Line.

Lieutenant W Kerr, Hawke Battalion, kil[l] in action 13 November, 19[

At 8.20am, Freyberg decided to consolidate the ground won and ordered the men to dig in about 150 yards short of the Yellow Line. His total force consisted of about 400 men and eleven Lewis gun crews. The 14/Worcesters, who were the Pioneers, were all casualties and there were practically no picks and shovels, so the men had to use their small entrenching tools. Freyburg signalled his intention to attack the village at 10.30am when the barrage was due to lift with 200 men and eight Lewis gun crews, but was informed that this event had been postponed because of the chaotic situation on the left, as

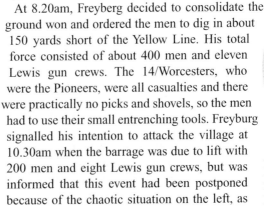

Lieutenant C A Edmondson, Hood Battalion, killed in action 13 November, 1916.

Sub Lieutena[n] A R Hart, H[Battalion, ki[in action 13 November, 1[

we have seen. So he and his men dug in and awaited the outcome of the 9.30am advance on the left. They waited all day. Fortunately, they had captured a German ration dump belonging to the 2/Guards Reserve Regiment and they were able to enjoy their cigars and dry socks and eat German cakes and sausages! Freyberg drank a large quantity of liquor in the afternoon before falling asleep out in the open, away from his shell hole and was 'rescued' later when his colleagues pulled him in by the legs. Contact was made on the right with 1/Cambridgshire Regiment of the 39th Division at Beaucourt Mill, where there was a river crossing. Much needed supplies were provided, especially bombs. Later, at 5.00pm, contact was also

The bridge over the Ancre where Freyberg's men were supplied by the 1/Cambridgeshire.

made with Commander Gilliland and his men on the left who had held on most of the day, isolated near the Beaucourt Road (Yellow Line) and who formed a defensive flank.

Gilliland recalled:

> *The very depleted force I had held on and under cover of darkness got in touch with the Hood Battalion on the right. No contacts were made on the left. I saw Colonel Freyberg and explained the position as it existed on the left of this battalion. In the morning I was wounded again and was unable to take any further part in the fighting.*

Darkness fell and Freyberg, who had been wounded twice, settled his men down for the night, frustrated that their progress had been held up as a result of the carnage around the redoubt, which remained uncaptured.

The Drake Battalion followed the Hood through the German wire, which had not been cut too effectively, but they passed through the gaps into the front line in small groups. Initially there was little sign of the enemy, Hood having cleared the way, and with whom some contact was made. In the second line though, in the locality of the redoubt, snipers were still active, especially on the left of the sector. It was here that Drake lost their commanding officer, Lieutenant Colonel A S Tetley, who went forward to see what was happening along with Lieutenant Commander P S Campbell. Both men were mortally

The view today of the station in the valley from where reinforcements arrived as the mist cleared.

Lieutenant Commander W Sterndale Bennett DSO.

wounded, Campbell hit three times before he succumbed. Several other officers were killed and wounded at about the same time and in the same position. The most senior officer remaining was Lieutenant Commander Sterndale Bennett but such was the ferocity of the German onslaught, little could be done to organise any further attack. The redoubt on the left had brought further very heavy fire to bear on the now mixed-up force of Drakes, some Hoods and a few Hawkes. On the right, though, the advance was able to make some progress through the German third line and was joined by some more men of the Hood and the 1/Honourable Artillery Company. As daylight came, this group could see the station ahead in the valley below to their right and changed direction half-right and, as we have seen, joined forces with Freyberg.

190 Brigade

The third wave of attacking battalions consisted of those belonging to 190 Brigade and their disposition was as follows, from left to right: The 10/Royal Dublin Fusiliers, 4/Bedfordshire Regiment, 7/Royal Fusiliers and the 1/Honourable Artillery Company.

1/Honourable Artillery Company, D Company, were allotted the task of defending the right flank of the Hood and were among the first to attack at zero hour. The company was split into two sections and one, in touch with the Hood on their right, occupied the ground in front of the Picturedrome, with the railway line on their right and the other, the far side of the railway at the Crow's Nest. Two Lewis gun crews were attached to the first section and one to the second, all provided by the 14/Worcesters.

At zero the left party charged with the Hoods and took the front line

68

with little opposition. Meanwhile, the party on the right crossed the area known as the Mound and entered the German trench at its extreme right and fought along it until the railway was reached. Here the 14/Worcesters' Lewis gun enfiladed the German bombers emerging from the top of the steep bank above the road; the second magazine wiped them out. This group were then held up by a German machine gun firing at them from a dugout further down the road towards the station. Because of the Worcesters' action the left party were able to get forward and the machine gun post was bombed from the top of the bank and the right party continued down the railway line towards the station, systematically fire bombing all the dugouts in the high bank and the railway embankment. Numerous prisoners were taken before they joined up with the other section of D Company at the German third line, the first objective. The advance made by Freyburg's men had been greatly assisted by these actions.

A Company of the 1/Honourable Artillery Company followed Freyberg during the initial stages of the advance and were busy clearing the dugouts that had been overlooked. Eventually they got in touch with the Hoods and Drakes ahead and dug in about 150 yards behind, but had no support on their left flank Later, some men of B Company arrived.Their advance had been hampered by the failure of the majority of the 7/Royal Fusiliers to make progress in front of the redoubt, which was still causing the whole of the advance to falter. C Company were held up with a detachment of the 7/Royal Fusiliers in the wire in front of the strongpoint, where Captain C S Rattigan, who was in command, was among the casualties. Snipers and machine guns were very busy. Then Captain Forster, taking over the 7/Royal Fusiliers, received orders that the redoubt was to be by-passed and a limited advance was made along the railway line and river bank.

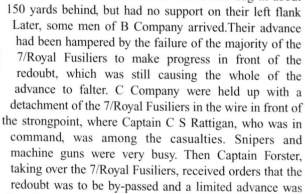
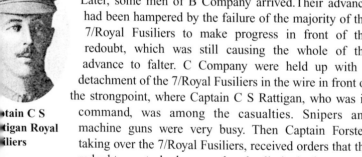

Captain C S Rattigan Royal Fusiliers

On the extreme left the 10/Royal Dublin Fusiliers and the 4/Bedfords could do little to support the Naval battalions in front of them and make progress much beyond the German second line. The 4/Bedfords had reported men held up in the second line at 10.40am and that they were taking heavy casualties. At 10.50am a brigade order to all units urged them to push on at all costs. At 11.00am the 1/Honourable Artillery Company and 7/Royal Fusiliers were ordered to send bombing parties either side of the redoubt from the rear so that the remainder of the 7/Royal Fusiliers could advance, but the attempt was abandoned.

At 12.22pm it was decided to send Captain Bastin of the Royal Marines, 190 Brigade Machine Gun Company and two sections of machine gunners into the German lines to attack the strongpoint, but it was an unequal contest, and coming under heavy fire, he was killed and his gun crews decimated. By 1.30pm the commanding officer of 4/Bedfords reported that he had gathered as many men together as he could and was trying to push forward, but there was great confusion in the deep mud. It is clear that late into the afternoon the Germans remained in force in their second and third lines, protected and resupplied from the redoubts which also dominated the front line and anyone trying to cross it. Meanwhile, messages were sent back to battalion and brigade headquarters urging the renewal of supplies, bombs, ammunition and water. In some cases reinforcements were asked for, including officers. When some arrived at Lieutenant Colonel Freyberg's position he told them to go back as he did not need them! There were not enough men to act as carrying parties and it was not until 6.30pm that 100 men left Hedauville, some miles behind the lines.

Finally, we look at the last battalion in the division, the 10/Royal Dublin Fusiliers, who were at the extreme left of the attack behind the Marine battalions. The battalion moved forward at zero hour into the trenches vacated by the Royal Marine battalions in front of them. At zero plus 46 minutes, they moved across in four waves and in the fog, keeping direction well, reached the sunken road with few casualties, although the German barrage was beginning to fall. However, within twenty-five yards of the German front line they were greeted by heavy machine-gun fire, especially from the left front. The left companies suffered particulary and there was no sign of the 51th (Highland) Division on their left. Men took shelter in shell holes alongside the dead and wounded of the Royal Marines. Second Lieutenant F O'Neill bravely led his platoon on through two lines of German defences and was about to jump into the third line when he was shot through the heart. His fellow officer, Lieutenant P McCusker, similarly charged, leading his platoon through the German front line. He was not seen again until his body was found in the German third line. He had been shot through the head. The Commanding Officer, Lieutenant Colonel E J St G Smith, attempted to get his battalion headquarters forward from Buckingham Palace Road into the German trenches, but he too was pinned down in No Man's Land. Here he met up with a section of the 190 Brigade Machine Gun Company led by Lieutenant Phillips. Smith spotted a gap to the right in the German wire and under cover of the machine guns, got through the gap into the front line with his

The Germans mount a counterattack.

headquarters staff, although he lost his Adjutant, Lieutenant Bailey.

Lieutenant Colonel Smith then reorganised all the men he could muster and sent Lieutenant McMahon and a party of men along the trench to the left to try and dislodge the Germans, who were holding up the advance there. McMahon and his men came upon a large German redoubt, similar to the one confronting the Hawke Battalion. It, too, was situated between the German Front and second lines. This one had four entrances in the front line and two each in the support and reserve lines. All the entrances concealed machine gun emplacements. The officer led his men bravely and effectively into a close-quarter attack on the machine gunners. Quite fortuitously, further to the left, Lieutenant Cox, on his own initiative, had gathered together a bombing party and some snipers and attacked simultaneously. The entrances in the front line were captured and the bombers threw in bombs before descending into its depths. Although capable of holding 1,500 men, most of its occupants were out defending the lines. It was mainly organised as a medical aid station and ammunition store. Its occupants, mostly medical staff and wounded men, soon surrendered.

The left of the attack was able to reorganise, although many officers had been lost, and push through to the second line. By now the time was 9.00am. Lieutenant Colonel Smith then moved his headquarters into the second line, but the situation was very confused with scattered parties of Bedfords, Royal Marines and Dublins. A strongpoint was established on the left and Smith made contact with Major Wiles of the 4/Bedfords and Lieutenant Colonel Cartwright and Lieutenant Colonel Hutchinson commanding 1/ and 2/Royal Marines. At midday orders came for all available men to be pushed forward. Because of the shortage of officers, the padre, Father S A L Thornton, went forward with a party of men supported by Sergeant T Priest and Sergeant J J McCormack and succeeded in capturing a group of seven Germans. These prisoners disclosed the whereabouts of a large dugout to Father Thornton, in which were sheltering from the British bombardment and trench mortars a battalion and its headquarters staff. The Germans led the padre and his men to the place where there was some initial firing and bomb-throwing after which Father Thornton went forward and called on the Germans to surrender. Some officers emerged and after talking to them, the priest persuaded them to do so, in spite of the German's potential numerical strength. Later, Father Thornton was observed leading over 400 men into captivity assisted by Sergeant McCormack, Sergeant Priest and about thirty men.

The attempted advance could not make progress against very heavy fire from the German third line, which was strongly held, although small groups did get through. Lieutenant Commander Sprange of the Howe Battalion, even though he was wounded got through to Station Road and even went as far as the Beaucourt Road, returning to report to Lieutenant Colonel Smith that although there were many snipers and some machine guns, there was no concerted opposition. Lieutenant Colonel Smith had no officers left. Lieutenant Cox was carried in badly wounded in the head. He had captured a party of Germans and was escorting them back when one of them threw a grenade at him. It was reported that some medical staff in a nearby dugout wished to surrender and Lieutenant Commander Sprange, who had remained to assist Lieutenant Colonel Smith, went to investigate and took possession of the dugout, which was then adopted as the Dublin's

Captured Germans assist in carrying a wounded soldier.

battalion headquarters. Later in the afternoon a lone runner arrived escorting twelve German prisoners who wished to surrender. A further order for all available men to be reorganised for an attack at 3.45pm failed to materialise. Darkness fell across the battlefield and on the left of the divisional attack, apart from the groups led by Lieutenant Colonel Freyberg and Commander Gilliland and other sundry groups and individuals, none of the six attacking battalions broke through. It was not even established that the enemy had been completely cleared from his front line and there was certainly resistance in parts of the second line. The third line was almost intact and heavily defended, while the remnants of six battalions lay decimated, mainly in front of the German wire.

Father Thornton, the Roman Catholic Padre, was attached to the Anson Battalion, Royal Naval Division, but these exploits are recorded in the diaries of the 10/Royal Dublin Fusiliers. It seems his duties extended across the 190 Brigade and the Masses he held would have been appropriate to many in the Royal Dublin Fusiliers, which may help to explain this. He was 46 years of age, and had lived and worked in Glasgow at St. Peter's College. A contemporary report said that he was an inspiration to all, always where he was most needed, in the front line. It was a remarkable sight to see this grey haired man driving himself forward in his gumboots through the mud, his spectacles balanced on the end of his nose. Soon after the battle he fell sick with stomach problems, having already had an operation for ulcers. Eventually in April 1917 he transferred to service in the Mediterranean. He died on 18 November 1936.

Rev. S A L Thornton in later life wearing his DSO.

The Roll Call

Lieutenant Colonel A H R Hutchinson was awarded the DSO as a result of this action

Lieutenant Colonel F J W Cartwright was awarded the DSO as a result of this action. He was wounded at Gavrelle Windmill and died on 30 April 1917 and is buried at Duisans Military Cemetery

Captain C L Muntz died of wounds on November 17 and is buried at Puchevillers Military Cemetery

Sub Lieutenant C G O Fletcher is buried in the Ancre British Cemetery

Lieutenant A F Maynard is commemorated on the Thiepval Memorial

Lieutenant C D F De la Mothe is buried in the Ancre British Cemetery

Lieutenant Colonel F J Saunders is buried in Hamel Military Cemetery

Lieutenant Commander J M Gilliland survived the war

Surgeon C H Gow is commemorated on The Thiepval Memorial

Lieutenant Commander B H Ellis was awarded the DSO. He was wounded in the neck while in command of the Hawke Battalion and died of wounds on 21 April 1918 and is buried in Wimereux Communal Cemetery

Commander W G Ramsay Fairfax was awarded the DSO. On 11 July 1917, he was declared unfit for active service owing to exhaustion and later went into the Tank Corps

Lieutenant H V Sewell is commemorated on the Thiepval Memorial

Lieutenant H B Van Praagh was the only unwounded officer in the 1 Royal Marine Battalion

Lieutenant R C G Edwards is commemorated on the Thiepval Memorial

Lieutenant D Jerrold survived his wounds and wrote about the Royal Naval Division after the war

Lieutenant The Honourable V S T Harmsworth is buried in the Ancre British Cemetery.

Surgeon J S Ward is commemorated on the Thiepval Memorial

Petty Officer J Elliott, Hawke Battalion is commemorated on the Thiepval Memorial.

Sub Lieutenant A P Herbert became a notable writer after the war

Lieutenant Colonel N O Burge is buried in Hamel Military Cemetery

Sub Lieutenant J H Emerson is buried in the Ancre British Cemetery

Lieutenant F S Kelly was awarded the DSO. He is buried in Martinsart Military Cemetery

Captain The Honourable S L Montague was awarded the DSO, survived the war and, as he predicted, named a racehorse Beaucourt

Lieutenant S H Fish was awarded the Military Cross. He was killed in action on the 25 August 1918 and is buried in Bucquoy Communal Extension Cemetery

Lieutenant Colonel A S Tetley is buried in Varennes Military Cemetery

Lieutenant Commander P S Campbell is buried in the Ancre British Cemetery

Lieutenant Commander W Sterndale Bennett was awarded the DSO. He died of wounds on November 7 1917 and is buried at Dozinghem Military Cemetery, Belgium

Captain C S Rattigan is commemorated on the Thiepval Memorial

Captain J Forster was awarded the Military Cross. He was killed in action on 2 October 1918 and is buried in the Sunken Road Cemetery, Boisleux St Marc

Captain E Bastin is buried in Y Ravine Cemetery, Beaumont Hamel

Lieutenant Colonel E J St. G Smith survived the battle but fell ill and was admitted to hospital. He was eventually sent home, where he was discharged from the army

Lieutenant J F Cox was awarded the Military Cross, survived his wounds but was invalided out of the army

Lieutenant V M McMahon was awarded the Military Cross. He was wounded on 6 January 1917 and never returned to active service.

Padre, Father S A L Thornton was awarded the DSO in January 1917

Sergeant J J McCormack was awarded the Military Medal. He was killed in action 17 February 1917 and is buried in Queens Cemetery, Bucquoy

Seargeant T Priest was killed in action on 11 February 1917 and is buried in the Ancre British Cemetery.

BROTHERS IN ARMS

The 10/Royal Dublin Fusiliers lost many of their officers as casualties during the attack that commenced on 13 November. Five were killed, a lower proportion than some of the other battalions, but by coincidence, two of these men had a common thread between them.

Second Lieutenant Frederick O'Neill was educated at Stoneyhurst College which he entered in 1891 at the age of twelve. Lieutenant Patrick McCusker was not yet born at that time and did not go to the school until 1903, when he was just nine years of age.

At the outbreak of war, O'Neill was working in South Africa, while McCusker was a medical student at Glasgow University. As we have seen, they were destined to die within a few yards of each other in the German third line.

Prior to the attack, in a dugout in the British reserve trench Fred O'Neill gave the address of his sister to a fellow officer and asked him to write to her and also go to see her if he was killed and his friend survived.

On the night of the 12th we lay out in the open and your brother had command of my leading platoon. He curled himself up in a shell hole and had a sleep. In the cold grey of the dawn...we advanced. There was a fog – a thick fog in fact – prevailing and I did not see Fred again. His death was instantaneous - shot through the heart – and the brave fellow's body was found lying before the German third line.

Patrick McCusker suffered an almost identical fate. His company commander wrote:

He was killed by a bullet to the head on November 13th 1916. It was the day our regiment advanced, and he fell leading his platoon. We found his body in the third German line and we buried him beside five of his brother

Lieutenant Frederick O'Neill (wearing cap-badge of Oxford and Bucks. Light Infantry. Below is Lieutenant P McCusker. They are buried together in Knightsbridge Cemetery.

officers who fell in the same action.

Padre Thornton wrote of 'Paddy' McCusker:

'A very good catholic, far and away the most devout in the whole battalion. Had he been forewarned that he was going to die he could not have made a better preparation...We left our billets on Sunday afternoon, to take our places for the push on Monday morning. On Sunday morning your son was at both Masses, and came up for Holy Communion and for absolution.

Padre, Rev S A Thornton in Ro⟨yal⟩ Naval Division uniform.

I never saw him again until I saw him lying dead, just as if he were asleep.

Of Fred O'Neill, Padre Thornton wrote:

He wasn't very long with us, but I had time to see that he was a very earnest, determined officer, and a good Catholic. He was at Mass on Sunday (the day before he died), received absolution and Holy Communion. He was as brave as a lion and died like a gallant gentleman, leading his men across 'No Man's Land' to the German trenches. I buried him with young McCusker in the same grave.

Chapter Four

ATTACK OF 39th DIVISION 13 NOVEMBER

The attack south of the River Ancre was co-ordinated to commence at the same time as that on the north bank. This may seem an obvious tactic, but it did not always occur, sometimes this was when there was more than a divisional boundary; for example, a corps boundary. This operation is interesting because it offered the opportunity to develop a different strategy and the situation was very successfully exploited.

The battalions taking part in the main attack were, moving from left

Map 9. The dispositions of the 39th Division, 13 November, 1916.

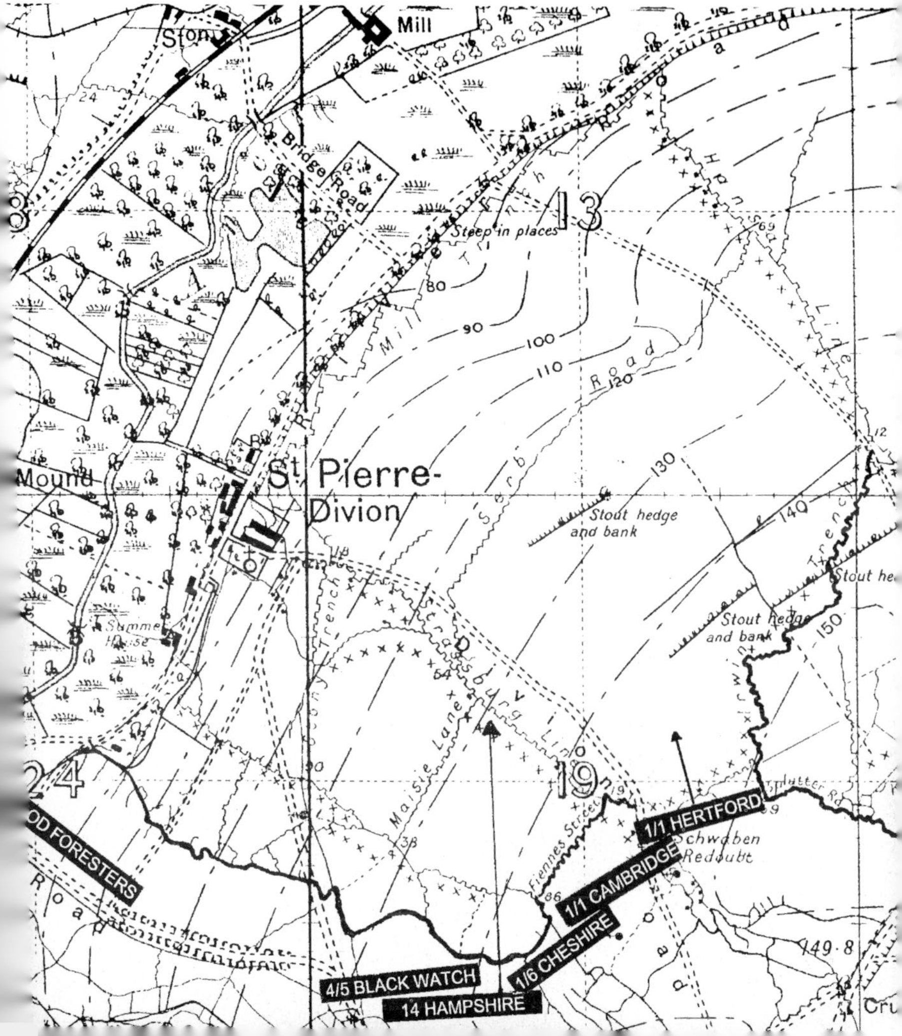

to right: the 4/5 Black Watch, 1/6 Cheshire, 1/1 Cambridgeshire and the 1/1 Hertfordshire. The 16/Sherwood Foresters were detached on the extreme left, opposite St Pierre Divion. The disposition of the troops and the starting points are as detailed on Map 9.

The ground, as already described, was extremely bad. Here, much effort was made to build wooden causeways or tracks from Thiepval Wood in the rear to enable men and equipment to get forward, otherwise everything and everybody would have just sunk. There were no obvious trenches to be seen, as these had collapsed and finding a location was very difficult. Great care was taken to assemble the troops without alerting the Germans to the imminent attack and this was completed successfully by 3.30am. Preparations had also been made by 118 Machine Gun Company who established eight gun positions near the Schwaben Redoubt so that enfilade fire could be directed onto the enemy's trenches on the north bank of the Ancre to aid the advance of the 63rd Division. Similarly, positions were made on the north bank by 116/Machine Gun Company to assist the 39th Division.

Before the assault, the 1/1 Hertfordshire, who were attacking through a gap in the German lines that had already been captured, moved forward to get across the old trench and look for better ground. This was detected by the Germans but went unchallenged. Their strength at the listening posts was thought not to be very strong or else they mistook the movement as wiring parties. This presented the 1/1 Hertfordshire with the opportunity to get in behind the Strasburg Line without a shot being fired. Three tanks had been allocated to the attack and special routes built to enable them to cross the terrain. One, however, still sank in the mud until it was hardly visible and another

Private A Fairweather, aged 30, 1 Cambridgeshire Regiment, was awarded the Military Medal, but was killed in action on 3 September 1917 exactly a year to the day of the attack.

broke a gear. The third, though, managed to get into position.

At zero hour, 5.45am, the fog was thick and direction was lost, especially on the left, although all officers had been given compass bearings. The 1/1 Hertfordshire, though, got away well and with open country ahead of them were at their objective, the Hansa Line by 7.00am. This position was heavily fortified. Fifty yards from the trench there was a belt of wire on 3 foot 6 inch metal screw pickets, six yards wide. Immediately in front of the trench, there was a similar barrier. Nevertheless, the men were soon into the trench near the point where it joined Mill Trench and broke through and also captured part of Mill Trench, nearly as far back as the junction of Bridge Road, all by 7.30am. They killed a great number of the enemy and took 140 prisoners. The 1/1 Cambridgeshire lost momentum at the start in the darkness and the fog, but two companies found the gap around the right hand side of the Strasburg Line and attacked the left of Mill Trench. The remaining companies were reorganised and soon followed. Mill Trench was reached at 7.15am and captured. By 11.30am the 1/1/Cambridgeshire arrived at the river bridge near Beaucourt Station and then went on to capture Beaucourt Mill linking up with Lieutenant Colonel Freyberg's men of the 63rd Division.

The two battalions on the left, the 1/6 Cheshire and the 4/5 Black Watch, were not to make a frontal approach to the German lines but to enfilade from the right and get between the German second and third

The Mill at Beaucourt.

lines. Once again, in the darkness, many men lost direction, became mixed up and lost in the maze of trenches and were unable to locate themselves accurately on the ground.

1/6 Cheshire

The 1/6 Cheshire advanced with four companies and the first waves of the attack made by A Company successfully reached the right of the Strasburg Line. Captain Kirk, commanding B Company, reached Maisie Lane, the first objective, but had lost touch with A Company and decided to wait in the mist and darkness to verify his position before moving on. Some men of the 4/5 Black Watch then joined his force which numbered about 200. At 6.51am D Company, led by Captain Innes, were the last to advance and on the way picked up C Company who had gone off in front but whose commander, Captain Dodge, and all other officers had been wounded. This combined force also arrived in Maisie Lane to find that Captain Kirk had been killed and Captain Innes assumed command of all three companies. At 8.00am Sergeant Hall arrived at battalion headquarters with the news that Captain Innes was now dead and there was no sign of A Company whatsoever.

The Adjutant, Lieutenant Naden, was sent forward at 8.15am with instructions to reassemble every man he could collect and push forward to the Strasburg Line and beyond to the Hansa Line. About 400 men were assembled and put under the command of a junior officer. At 8.45am, Lieutenant Naden confirmed by telephone that this force had moved forward in four waves. The Strasburg Line was still holding out, though, in many sections and the 14/Hampshire in support were called forward to clear it out.

Contact was then made for the first time with A Company, who reported that they had reached the right of the Hansa Line and were taking prisoners and were in touch with the 1/1 Cambridgeshire. At 9.00am a message was received from Lieutenant Yorston who asked for assistance as he was pinned down in Serb Trench with twelve men and under attack. Soon afterwards the advancing parties sent forward by Lieutenant Naden reached the position and drove the attackers off. Just after 9.30am reports were received that St Pierre Divion had fallen and that the Strasburg Line was finally cleared.

4/5 Black Watch

The advance was made with four companies. The precise formation is not known, but it is clear that in the conditions direction was soon lost and information was very sparse. Only five messages were received at battalion headquarters all day in connection with the advance and three of these came from Captain Plimpton commanding A Company. At 6.25am he reported that he was at the first objective (the original German front line) but had become isolated and had lost touch with D Company on his left and also the 1/6 Cheshire on his right. At 7.30am Captain Plimpton sent a message that he was now in a position between the German front and second line and had captured two dugouts full of Germans but was still isolated. By 9.00am, he was in the Strasburg Line and in touch with C Company on his left. Another eighty prisoners had been taken and a machine gun captured and he was about to advance towards the Hansa/Mill Trench objective. He also reported that a tank was stuck in the German second line. B Company was led by Captain Stevenson, who was wounded, but nothing was heard of this company until an untimed message was received stating that Lieutenant Bell and ten men had joined the 1/6 Cheshire in the Hansa Line. Lieutenant Murray was in command of C Company and reported that soon after zero he had lost direction and was attempting to reorganise and push on. Thereafter no further news was received and no contact at all was made with D Company, led by Second Lieutenant McCririck, who was wounded.

16/Sherwood Foresters

The remaining battalion in the attack advanced astride the St Pierre Divion Road. They broke through the German front line, one company attacking along the top of the bank, while the other concentrated on the road below it and attacked the dugouts and tunnels under the bank. The German garrison consisted of the 38th Division and units of the Sherwood Foresters broke through into one of the larger tunnel entrances. To their surprise they found electric lights showing the way forward, but these were soon extinguished. Some hand torches were produced, but the air was very foul and it was decided to withdraw.

As the troops approached the German second line, many emerged from their dugouts and mounted a determined and heavy bombing counterattack. Eventually they were driven back underground and the dugouts were bombed and sentries posted. On top of the bank the Foresters' right company was also attacked with bombs and a reserve company had to be called forward to assist and the attack was driven off. This seems to have been the final show of defiance and with its failure and with most of the tunnels blocked, many Germans emerged into the open in the village and surrendered. The German battalion Headquarters was captured and very soon the number of prisoners far

British and French troops sort through German equipment at St Pierre Divion.

exceeded those of the Sherwood Foresters, who had been joined by some men of the 4/5 Black Watch. The time was then 9.00am. By 11.30am, the whole of the Hansa Line had been penetrated and cleared, and the 1/1 Hertfordshire were establishing new defensive positions about fifty yards to the east of this trench which was to be utilised as the British second line. In case of a counterattack they built a strongpoint on top of the bank where the Hansa Line joined the St Pierre Divion – Grandcourt Road and, in view of the uncertainty on the north side of the river and further down the road towards Grandcourt, the whole village was ringed with new defensive positions and strongly wired. The sole tank involved in the battle advanced across the German front line and was attacked and surrounded, and its officer was killed. The rest of the crew beat off their opponents and

A pigeon is released from a tank.

continued, driven by Corporal Taffs, but when it reached the German second line at about 8.00am, it crashed through the top of a dugout and fell on its side and was attacked again. A pigeon safely delivered a message for assistance, but meanwhile a party of Sherwood Foresters, assisted later by some men of the Black Watch drove the Germans off.

There was no serious counterattack; the Germans seem to have wholly underestimated the extent of the assault and its timing, and continued to do so when at about 6.45pm on the evening of 13 November they sent a party of twenty-five men, including an officer and five machine guns to capture the strongpoint. They were all killed or captured and every gun was taken. Later another party of twenty men tried to rush the post with a similar outcome. Again, on the evening of 14 November, a party of twenty bombers were nearly all killed.

There is no doubt that the success of this operation assisted the progress of the 63th Division, particularly on the right of their attack, where, as we have seen, progress was made to Beaucourt Station. In previous attacks heavy fire had been directed from Mill Trench and the dugouts at St Pierre Divion. In this operation the large majority of troops seem to have arrived at various points along Mill Trench and at St Pierre Divion, but not necessarily at the intended place. Only the 1/6 Cheshire made a direct frontal attack on the Hansa Line together with some of the 1/1 Cambridgeshire, although the strength and exact location of these are not known. The initial breakthrough was made by the 1/1 Hertfordshire, and with the subsequent surrender in the village, this would have left any occupants of the Hansa Line further to the right totally isolated and cut off on both flanks; the probability is that they surrendered or retreated to the rear. The 4/5 Black Watch were ordered to relieve the 1/1 Cambridgeshire in the Hansa Line, much to the obvious displeasure of their commanding officer who wrote;

When it is considered that the battalion had attacked at dawn and advanced a thousand yards, that companies were greatly disorganised, that many men had got mixed up with other units and the new line to be held was roughly a mile from the position the battalion was in when the orders were received, the difficulty of carrying out this operation successfully will be easily recognised.

On the face of it, it would appear to be hard on the men as they had experienced a difficult time in the German front lines and had to call up every officer left in the battalion. Many reinforcements were called forward, supplies of all kinds had to be dragged over the appalling terrain and the relief was not completed until midnight.

The Roll Call

Captain R Kirk was awarded the Military Cross. He is buried in Lonsdale Cemetery, Authuille

Captain W R Innes is buried in Lonsdale Cemetery, Authuille

Captain R A Plimpton was awarded the Military Cross and Bar. He was killed in action 27 September 1917. He is commemorated on Tyne Cot Memorial, Belgium

Captain T Stevenson was awarded the Military Cross and Bar. He was killed in action exactly a year to the day of this attack, on 14 November 1917. He is buried in La Clytte Military Cemetery, Reninghelst, Belgium

Corporal Taffs survived the war

German prisoners taken on 13 November in St Pierre Divion.

Chapter Five

TUESDAY 14 NOVEMBER

In the afternoon of the 13 November orders were issued that would bring yet another four battalions into the fray. The 10/Royal Fusiliers, 13/Royal Fusiliers, 13/King's Royal Rifle Corps and 13/Rifle Brigade constituted the 111 Brigade of the 37th Division and they had been ordered to move up and be in position to attack on the morning of 14 November.

During the night of 13/14, sporadic attacks and fighting continued into the night through until about 4.00am, as groups of men from the Royal Marines, Bedfords, Royal Dublins and others, isolated in the German defensive system, attempted to get forward to the Green Line. As we already know, some did advance in the darkness and were able to make contact, especially on the left, with the 51st Division. The main battle, though, was to be fought on the right of the sector, where Lieutenant Colonel Freyberg was waiting.

The 13/King's Royal Rifle Corps and the 13/Rifle Brigade marched up from Mesnil during the afternoon of the 13 November and reached

Map 10. The final assault on Beaucourt village.

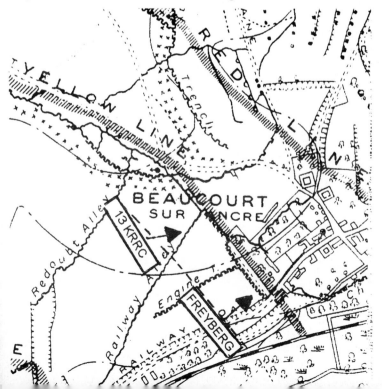

the battle area at 9.30pm. Their orders were to extend the left of Lieutenant Colonel Freyberg's troops and get as close to the Beaucourt Road (Yellow Line) as possible. However, some confusion occurred when the 13/Rifle Brigade stopped at Station Road (Green Line) and the 13/King's Royal Rifle Corps continued alone, in file, along the road to Beaucourt village to meet up with Freyberg. After discussions, it was arranged that the 13/King's Royal Rifle Corps were to clear and occupy the ground to the left and scouts were sent out, led by Lieutenant F S Pemberton, and bombing parties were organised by Second Lieutenant R G Humphreys. About fifty prisoners were taken and the line extended as far as Redoubt Alley. This ground was then occupied by C and D Companies, but their left flank was unexpectedly exposed.

The attack had been planned to take place in two stages. At 6.00am it was intended to occupy and consolidate the whole of the Yellow Line and then at 7.45am launch the final assault on Beaucourt village and establish the Red Line beyond it. The confusion in the orders was cleared up when it was established that at 6.00am, the 13/Royal Fusiliers would come up on the left of the 13/King's Royal Rifle Corps and the 13/Rifle Brigade, who had also arrived in Station Road overnight, would further extend the line to the left. At 6.20am that advance on the left began and the 13/Rifle Brigade and the 13/Royal Fusiliers attacked from Station Road trench with the objective of taking the rest of the Beaucourt Road (Yellow Line). By 7.00am, elements of the 13 Royal Fusiliers joined up on the left of the 13/King's Royal Rifle Corps, but the 13/Rifle Brigade were held up and could get

Flooding in the Ancre Valley.

no nearer than 200 yards from Beaucourt Road. The left of the main attack had, however, been extended by a further 300 yards.

On the right, Lieutenant Colonel Freyberg, it will be recalled, had occupied the Yellow Line on the edge of Beaucourt village but had been forced to withdraw and had dug in about 150 yards further back to wait. The plan was for the 1/Honourable Artillery Company to advance at 6.00am from Beaucourt Station and pass through Freyburg's mixed force and occupy the Yellow Line prior to a final assault on the village at 6.45am.

The night had been very cold and, again, a mist covered the battlefield and the mud sapped what energy the men had left. Some of the men of the 1/Honourable Artillery Company were reported as being near exhaustion and there is no reason to think that men of other battalions were in any better condition. The exception would have to be the battalions of 111 Brigade who had only left their billets in Hedauville the previous day.

It is not possible to give an accurate figure of the number of men Lieutenant Colonel Freyberg had at his disposal that morning. Where numbers are given, they sometimes vary depending on the source. It is safe to say, however, that he had between 700 and 800. His own mixed force numbered about 300, and there were between 300 and 400 1/Honourable Artillery Company and eighty-seven Royal Fusiliers. On his left, the numbers of the 13/Kings Royal Rifle Corps are unknown but if we follow the general pattern of events and assume that they, as with all the other battalions, were understrength by about a third, an additional 500 would have been assembled.

The advance of the 1/Honourable Artillery Company at 6.00am behind Freyberg's men came under heavy attack and faltered. Men took shelter in shell holes and those that made it forward to join Freyberg found the trench his men had been forced to dig with their small entrenching tools shallow and crowded. Some men had made it forward towards the Yellow Line but were pinned down in shell holes. The situation was quite chaotic.

13/King's Royal Rifle Corps

On the left of the village, dug in short of the Yellow Line, C and D Companies, commanded by Captain Procter and Captain Stocks, were the closest to the village, but were being hampered by the British barrage falling short. Captain Procter's company was on the right. The attack was due to commence at 7.30am and the plan was to move to the right, initially, and make a frontal assault on the village. No details of

Petty Officer R Laidlaw, Hawke Battalion, was awarded the Military Medal. He killed twenty-six Germans in one dugout himself.

the attack on the right by Freyberg seem to have been given to the company commanders.

Five minutes before the attack Sergeant Gosling of C Company went over to Captain Stocks and told him there were no officers left in his company. All had been hit by a British shell, with Second Lieutenant Holmes killed and all the others seriously wounded. Lieutenant Hawkins arrived to take over C Company and the plan of attack was changed. A machine gun in Beaucourt Road (Yellow Line) had been trained on C Company's front for most of the morning but, further to the left, D Company were largely unhindered. Captain Stocks, therefore, decided to take this position from a half right approach and attack its flank with his men. Fortuitously, there was a trench directly in front of his position which had not been blocked and which provided a covered approach towards the machine gun. As soon as the barrage lifted, Captain Stocks gave the order to advance, some men going up the trench while others rushed across the open. Beaucourt Road was taken with hardly a blow being struck, large groups of Germans walked across in the open with their hands up and the edge of the village was reached at about 8.00am. Lieutenant Hawkins' C company also reached the village and Captain Stocks asked him to move his men to the right as he was crowding his company unduly. This resulted in a gap opening up but this was filled by a section of A Company led by Second Lieutenant Dawe, who cleared some houses. When about half way through the village, Lieutenant Hawkins became a casualty.

Meanwhile, with Freyberg, the 1/Honourable Artillery Company made two further attempts to get forward but without success. Reports came through that on the left the 13/King's Royal Rifle Corps were on the outskirts of the village, and Freyberg, leading from the front and exposing himself to great danger, reorganised the men. Although wounded again, he led the whole force forward which, with a great cheer, succeeded in entering Beaucourt with a frontal attack. Captain The Honourable S L Montague, writing later, described how waiting in the trench behind Freyberg he saw him jump out of his trench and wave the men on. At first few followed, the bullets were 'raining past us' and one ripped through his sleeve as he followed Freyberg. Suddenly Freyberg fell, a bullet hit his helmet and knocked him over, but he got up and continued. Clambering through some wire a German threw a grenade at him and he was wounded for a third time.

Unlike some of the front line villages, such as Beaumont-Hamel,

Beaucourt sur l'Ancre had not been turned into a 'fortress', but there were plenty of dugouts and shelters from which many Germans emerged without a fight and surrendered. There was some resistance, however, from bombers and snipers, some of the latter from across the valley on the right and the 39th Division were sent messages to this effect. The advance of the 13/King's Royal Rifle Corps was held up at one point by a fusilade of bombs thrown unexpectedly at very short range from a concealed dugout. The advance faltered, but Rifleman Sweet and Rifleman Bailey, acting with great courage, held their ground and countered with Mills bombs, although both were wounded. Lance Corporal Hinder, who had a Lewis gun, dropped his weapon and rushed back for more bombs and succeeded in completing the operation. Thereafter, any resistance was normally overcome by a few doses of fire from the Lewis gun.

The forces in the village once again became mixed up but, by 9.00am, Freyberg set about organising its defence from counterattack. Lines of defence were established from the River Ancre valley on the extreme right, across to the left, where the situation on the divisional boundary with the 51st Highland Division was unclear. This line was east of the village and crossed the Beaucourt – Miraumont road in front of Baillescourt Farm. It is not possible to be quite sure as to the disposition of the troops on this defensive line as they are not specifically given. Certainly, the 13/King's Royal Rifle Corps, commanded by Captain Stocks, were on the left and, from the descriptions of the ground, some of the 1 Honourable Artillery Company were dug in immediately in front of the village across the Miraumont Road with other men of the Royal Naval Division on the right in the Ancre valley, to the railway and beyond where there were also some more representatives of the 1/Honourable Artillery Company. Freyberg set up battalion headquarters in a house in the village and settled down. Suddenly, a barrage of howitzers opened up and seemed to be ranging on the house. Everyone scattered as all equipment and the house itself was blown to bits. Freyburg, together with Montague, ran to a trench in the open occupied by the 1/Honourable Artillery Company. A German counterattack was thought to be imminent. The men in the trench were half buried several times by

Surgeon W McCracken, DSO and Bar, Hood Battalion. He was also recommended for the Victoria Cross. After the war he went into General Practice in the Brönte village of Haworth in West Yorkshire, where he remained for forty years.

earth and stones and then a shell fell very close. Montague, who had a wounded man lying on him, was slightly wounded himself when he heard Freyberg call out, 'Goodbye Montague' and then 'Steady Hood!' which is the battalion's motto. He looked a very bad colour and was bleeding profusely from a wound to the neck. The shell fragment had stripped the flesh on the back of his neck to the vertebrae and he lost consciousness. After about half an hour he came to. The shell that wounded him killed two men, one either side of him and further wounded the 1/Honourable Artillery Company man lying on Montague. After a while Freyberg got up and asked Montague to take him to the dressing station, which, although only 300 yards away was quite an ordeal. Montague recalled the sad pleas of the badly wounded on the way, begging for help.

Montague then took over command of the Hood Battalion until it was withdrawn later that evening. Overall command passed to the Commanding Officer of the 13/King's Royal Rifle Corps, Lieutenant Colonel Chester-Master. The only battalion involved in the final capture of Beaucourt not relieved after the battle was the 13/King's Royal Rifle Corps, who remained in the front line for a further five days. Chester-Master was moved to send the following message:

> *I consider that it is my duty to report that my medical officer informed me last night that the health of my battalion has suffered considerably as a result of the exposure to cold, lack of sleep and stress of the last few days which have brought many of them to a point of exhaustion from which it will take many weeks to recuperate. He therefore warns me that they are no longer physically capable of doing themselves justice in an emergency or if called upon to make a special effort. I do not wish this report to be taken as an appeal for relief.*

While all this was happening, drastic action had to be taken to dislodge the occupants of the redoubt who were still holding out opposite the front of the Hawke attack. Major General Shute ordered three tanks to be sent forward from Auchonvillers during the night of 13/14 November. They were met by Lieutenant A. Campbell, who got into the first tank and steered it himself towards the objective. They crossed the British front line somewhere near the sunken road and, taking advantage of the downward slope, travelled southwards along No Man's Land looking for a suitable place to cross into the German lines. Almost immediately one tank was knocked out by a shell, but the remaining two continued through the mud and one successfully crossed the German front line but then became stuck. The other tank became stuck on the British side of

the German lines. They were, however near enough to the redoubt to be observed by its occupants and a few rounds of the six pounder guns was enough to encourage surrender and a white flag was waved. Nothing seemed to happen, though, and no Germans appeared. The crews in the tanks then got out of their machines and, armed with Hotchkiss guns, advanced on the enemy who at once gave themselves up and two officers and 400 men emerged.

Lieutenant A Campbell, was attached to the Trench Mortar Battery, but came forward to steer the tank against the Redoubt, for which action he was awarded the Military Cross.

That night, Captain Montague arrived at the redoubt with his men where they were to spend the night. He recalled the area was full of gruesome sights. Many dead were strewn around; some had arms and legs missing, their faces sometimes blown away. Having been without sleep for three days he managed to get a few hours in a bunk within the depths of its shelter, although he was compelled to share this privilege with a dead German.

The redoubt, when it was fully explored, was found to be three stories deep and had wire beds and mattresses for three hundred men. There were entrances in No Man's Land and also from the first, second and third line trenches and there was one facing Station Road up which a light railway had been run. It consisted of innumerable small rooms, officers messes, kitchens and store rooms, all of which were scattered with clothing, food and equipment all hurriedly abandoned. One room was an aid post and a model of its kind, lined with red canvas, lit with electric light and replete with innumerable splints, bandages, instruments and drugs. Opening out of this was a ward with twelve beds. The officers mess

A German casualty.

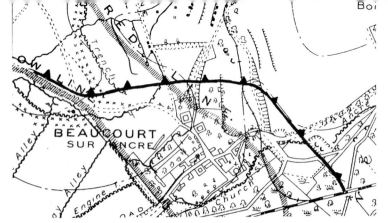

Map 11. The position in front of the village as reported by the 13 KRRC. Note how this differs from the red line shown on the map.

was lined with tasteful red wallpaper and pictures, a gilt mirror, mahogany table and comfortable red plush chairs. There was also a well filled wine cellar and well appointed kitchen.

Within a few days, the Somme offensive was called off. It is not within the scope of this book to discuss the merits of the campaign except to record that the objectives set had proved optimistic. The battle had lasted from 1 July until 18 November, a total of 141 days. The British and Commonwealth casualties alone amounted to nearly 420,000, about 3,000 day. Most accounts refer to Lieutenant Colonel Freyberg as being wounded three times, twice by British artillery fire and finally while taking shelter at Beaucourt. A fourth event has been included, when he was hit by a grenade, but not seriously enough to impede his progress, it seems.

It would not be appropriate to leave the narrative of the achievements of the Royal Naval Division without mention of the fate of Lieutenant E L A Dyett, Nelson Battalion, aged twenty-one. This

German machine guns captured at Beaucourt-sur-Ancre.

officer was subsequently court martialled and executed for alleged desertion. Much has already been recorded about this, and there is no point in repeating the details of this tragedy here. An account of this appears in the *Beaumont Hamel* edition of this series, and also in *Shot at Dawn* written by Sykes and Putkowski. Nevertheless, it was the one incident that cast a cloud over the events recorded here, and still provokes controversy today.

The Roll Call

Lieutenant F S Pemberton survived the war

Second Lieutenant R G Humphreys was killed in action on 28 September 1917 and is commemorated on Tyne Cot Memorial, Belgium

Captain J Stocks was awarded the Military Cross and survived the war

Second Lieutenant E C Holmes is buried in Hamel Military Cemetery

Second Lieutenant G W Hawkins was taken back to Hamel, arriving on 15 November, when he was already dead, and was buried in Hamel Military Cemetery

Second Lieutenant A H Dawe was killed in action 11 April 1917 and is commemorated on the Arras Memorial

Rileman L Sweet was killed in action 24 August 1918 and is buried in Bienvillers Military Cemetery

Lance Corporal G Hinder was promoted to Corporal. He was killed in action 28 February 1917 and is buried in Philosphe British Cemetery, Mazingarbe

Lieutenant Commander A Campbell was awarded the Military Cross. He was killed by shellfire at Welsh Ridge, Cambrai, 30 December 1917 and is buried at Metz-en-Couture Communal Cemetery, British Extension

Lieutenant Colonel R C Chester-Master DSO & Bar had been a career soldier, but retired and joined the police. At the outbreak of war, he was Chief Constable of Gloucestershire, but resigned to re-enlist. He was killed in action 30 August 1917 and is buried in Locre Hospice Cemetery, Belgium.

THREE VICTORIA CROSSES

The pages in this book briefly record the exploits of three recipients of the Victoria Cross. Much has already been written of this and the book *VCs of the Somme* by Gerald Gliddon has much information and detail and there is no purpose in repeating it here except to record:

Lieutenant Geoffrey St George Shillington Cather, 9/Royal Irish Fusiliers, was Adjutant of the battalion and after the failed attack of 1 July went out into No Man's Land to help the wounded. He continued to bring men in and it was during the morning of 2 July that he was shouting to anyone who was able to respond in an effort to locate wounded men.

Lieutenant G St G S Cather VC.

Colonel Blacker wrote later:

He heard a man calling out and went over the parapet in broad daylight and gave him water, called out to see if there was anyone else within hail, saw a hand waving feebly, went on and was shot through the head by a machine gun and was killed instantaneously.

His remains were never found and identified and he is commemorated on the Thiepval Memorial to the Missing.

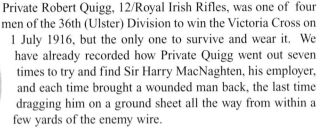

Private Robert Quigg, 12/Royal Irish Rifles, was one of four men of the 36th (Ulster) Division to win the Victoria Cross on 1 July 1916, but the only one to survive and wear it. We have already recorded how Private Quigg went out seven times to try and find Sir Harry MacNaghten, his employer, and each time brought a wounded man back, the last time dragging him on a ground sheet all the way from within a few yards of the enemy wire.

Robert Quigg survived the war and lived in a cottage on the MacNaghten estate until May 1955, aged seventy, when he died. He was buried at Billy Parish Church.

Rifleman R Quigg VC.

Lieutenant Colonel Bernard Cyril Freyberg was born in Surrey, but his parents emigrated to New Zealand when he was barely two years of age. He was something of an adventurer and was twenty-five years old at the outbreak of war when he joined the Royal Naval Division. He had previously been awarded the DSO in the early stages of the Gallipoli campaign for swimming across the Gulf of Xeros and back to his ship again after lighting flares on the shore to deceive the enemy into thinking a landing had taken place. He was a pallbearer at the funeral of Rupert Brooke who had also been an officer in the Hood Battalion.

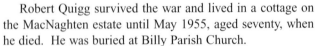

We have already recorded how Freyberg won his Victoria Cross and his subsequent and colourful career is charted in Gliddon's book. He died in 1963 aged seventy-four, having been Governor of Windsor Castle for eleven years. He is buried at St Martha's Church, Chilworth, Surrey, where his headstone simply states 'Bernard Freyberg VC 1889 – 1963'.

Lieutenant Colonel B Freyber DSO VC

Chapter Six

VISITING THE BATTLEFIELDS

It should be possible to complete a visit to the area using only the maps contained within this book. However, if preferred, and especially if visits to other parts of the battlefields are intended, there are good maps available. The yellow Michelin 1/200,-000 (1cm-:2km) series give good detail and will guide you on your journey south from Calais and around the area. The numbers required are 51 and 52. The Commonwealth War Graves Commission produce these with an overprint of all the war cemeteries and an index. Sometimes, though, it is difficult to read the map as there so many of them. There is also the larger Serie Bleue IGN maps (1cm-250m). The map covering this book is 2407 O, Acheux-en-Amienois. To cover the majority of the battlefields you will need another three maps, 2407 E, 2408 O and 2408 E. All these maps can be purchased at Maison de la Presse in Albert, which is on the left of the square as you stand on the steps at the west end of the Basilique.

The quickest route to the Somme is to cross from Dover to Calais (or Folkestone to Calais via the Shuttle). From Calais follow the signs for the A26 to Arras and Paris. The autoroute will be quiet. Continue to the junction of the A26/A1, continuing to follow the signs to Paris. As you join the A1 the traffic will be heavier but the journey is only a short one to Exit 16 for Bapaume. The distance from Calais is about 90 miles. From Bapaume take the D929 to Albert.

The dead await burial.

You should book your accommodation in advance. Although the growth in numbers of those visiting the battlefields has been reflected in an increase in available accommodation, an imbalance still exists. Remember the area is rural and agricultural, the nearest large hotels are in Amiens or Arras.

If you have nowhere to stay, call at the Office du Tourisme in Albert. This is opposite the Basilique, towards the right. The staff there speak English. I have included a selective list of accommodation as an appendix to this section to assist the reader in making an advance booking.

What you need to have in your luggage will depend on what time of year you decide to visit. Winter can be cold on the Somme and wet too! Full waterproofs, together with wellingtons or good boots are essential. Warm clothing should include gloves and headwear. A day sack is also useful to put in your camera, small first aid kit, penknife, bottle opener, corkscrew and refreshments, books, maps, pens and other bits and pieces. Summer can still present wet conditions, even though the average rainfall is less than in Britain. It can also be considerably hotter in summer, and temperatures can soar above 30°C or more. Protection in the form of headwear and sun cream is essential. Always have available plenty to drink, not necessarily alcohol for that can be counterproductive in more ways than one.

Driving in the Somme should present few problems. The roads, with a few exceptions, are much quieter and in this area you are as likely to meet a British registered car as a French one. There are some important differences to remember and the first and most important one is to remember to drive on the right. The most dangerous time is when first setting out after a halt. It is very easy to pull out on to the left of the carriageway with potentially disastrous results.

The cheapness and availability of alcohol together with the distance from home, should not lure the visitor into believing it is alright to drink and drive. The alcohol limit is lower than at home in Britain (50 milligrams) and it is rigorously enforced by regular road blocks for mass on-the-spot testing and there is no escape!

It is also a legal requirement to carry a warning triangle and a set of replacement light bulbs. All documents should be carried too; this includes, insurance, driving licence and registration document. Your insurance should include full European Cover, obtainable through your insurance company. Failure to do this could result in your being insured for only third party under current EU law. Breakdown insurance is a matter for your own judgement. There are several garages in Albert who act as agents for most popular makes of cars and I know several instances of their services being well received.

The final point on motoring is to beware of the rule 'Priority from the Right'. In all cases, unless marked otherwise, you must give way to the traffic approaching anywhere from the right. This includes traffic approaching you ostensibly from ahead but offset to the right. In the country, the sign to look for is a cross (X) which normally indicates priority from the right at the next junction. If you have priority the junction will normally be marked with broken lines, as at home, or there will be a road sign with a pointed arrow with a bar through it. In urban areas, unless marked otherwise, all junctions are priority from the right.

As a member of the EU, the UK has a reciprocal arrangement with France and other European member countries for obtaining medical treatment. By obtaining forms E111 from any Post Office, you will be able to take advantage of this but in the case of France, this falls well short of what you can expect at home. In the first place, you may be asked for money 'up front.' Treatment and any drugs must be paid for and then claimed back in the same way that a French national is required to do from the local social security office. Only a proportion of the costs will be refunded – between 60% and 80%. Medical treatment can be expensive and the claimant could still be presented with a substantial bill. It should also be remembered that such things as re-arranged hotel and travel expenses or repatriation are not covered. No special inoculations are necessary but it is advisable to have tetanus injections. The Somme is a high risk area; because of its history, all agricultural workers are obliged to have injections. There are many agencies offering travel insurance – a few pounds for a few days would seem a reasonable investment. There are also now annual policies and these are good value for money which offer an unlimited number of trips.

Always have your passport with you. The French have a national identity card and the Gendarmes and Police could ask you to provide proof of identity. The Somme region is a quiet, and on the whole, a trouble free area but crime does exist. Be careful not to leave valuables in your car. There have been instances of British cars being broken into while the owners were away walking or visiting a distant cemetery.

Albert is the largest centre of population, most of the soldiers involved in the fighting on the Somme would be familiar with it. It was a garrison town just behind the British lines and was regularly shelled by German artillery. Its most famous landmark is the Madonna and

The Basilque in Albert as it looked in 1917.

Child on top of the Basilque which hung precariously for most of the duration of the war. It was said at the time that when it fell the war would end. Many years later, a veteran friend of mine, Alan Walmsley of the Duke of Wellington's Regiment, was always sceptical about the legend of the Golden Virgin. With his dry northern sense of humour he said, 'That couldn't be right, you know, 'cos the bloody Royal Engineers wired it up!' Today it stands above the town and shines out at night, a beacon which can be seen from many points across the surrounding countryside.

The floodlighting was renewed in 1996 as part of the Commemoration of the 80th Anniversary of the Battle of the Somme. In 2000, a fuller renovation of the building was commenced and it is now pristine and gleaming in its gold paint. It is in Albert where most visitors do their shopping and buy fuel. There is an interesting underground museum dedicated to the First World War. It is housed in tunnels used as shelters during the Second World War and the entrance is signposted near the west end of the Basilique.

Finally, the visitor to the Somme will almost certainly come across

Vic Simpson (left) and Alan Walmsley, both Duke of Wellington's, meet again for the first time since the War (1988).

the debris of war. Although recently there have been renewed efforts to clear up live shells, hand grenades and mortar bombs as they come to light, there are still many of these potentially lethal objects about. It is as well to remember that the cemeteries we visit and memorials we look at represent tens of thousands killed by these explosives and the increase in 'accidents' in recent years has caused the authorities to take certain steps to reduce the risk of injury or death. It is now forbidden to possess anything - even a simple .303 cartridge - that is live. It is also forbidden to possess anything that has been defused and to possess a metal detector. If you do come across any human remains, the first action should be to report it to the local Gendarmes. The Commonwealth War Graves Commission at Beaurains, near Arras, will not normally attend unless called by the Gendarmes, but assistance could be sought from the local teams of the Commission's workers who will be seen frequently about the area. The nearest workbase is at the Thiepval Memorial and there is also one at the hamlet of Serre.

WHERE TO STAY

Listed Hotels in Albert
***Royal Picardie, Route d'Amiens 80300
Tel (0033) 322753700 ~ Fax (0033) 322756019

**La Basilique, 3 Rue Gambetta 80300
Tel (0033) 322750471 ~ Fax (0033) 322751047

*Hotel de la Paix, 39 Rue Victor Hugo 80300
Tel (0033) 322750164 ~ Fax (0033) 322754417

Listed Chambres d'Hôtes (Bed & Breakfast)

These three are very local and within walking distance of the area covered in the book.

*Nr Beaumont Hamel Les Galets, Route de Beaumont,
Tel (0033) 322762879 Auchonvillers 80560 ~ Fax (0033) 322762879

Grandcourt, 9 Rue de Beaucourt 80300
Tel (0033) 322748158 ~ Fax (0033) 322748158

*Auchonvillers, Avril Williams Guesthouse,
Tel (0033) 322762366 ~ 10 Rue Delattre, 80560

*These are British owned establishments.

Other Recommended Establishments

There are few facilities in the battlefield area itself for the tourist. However those looking for refreshment or somewhere to have a meal will find the following satisfactory:

Auberge de la Valleé d'Ancre
A good quality restaurant at reasonable prices
6 Rue Moulin, Authuille 80300 ~ Tel 0322751518

Le Poppy
A cheap but good 'Les Routiers' style restaurant
4 Route Bapaume, Ovillers 80300 ~ Tel 0322754545

Le Tommy
Bar, cafeteria and trench museum
Rue Albert, Pozieres ~ Tel 0322748284

Ulster Memorial Tower
Thiepval. Light refreshments and toilets ~ Tel Offfice 0322748111
Public 0322748714

Newfoundland Park
Beaumont Hamel. Toilets available ~ Tel 0322762022

Delville Wood, Longueval
Light refreshments and toilets. South African Memorial and Museum
~ Tel 0322850217

WALKS AND TOURS: INTRODUCTION

As mentioned elsewhere in this book, this area is more interesting than some other parts of the Somme Battlefield in that the topographical features are well defined. The Ancre valley forms the most prominent, but with other smaller valleys or re-entrants existing both north and south of the river that have not changed sinced the action that took place in November 1916. No amount of ploughing or other agricultural activity can change that, but some changes have taken place. Looking at older photographs it is possible to see more trees and hedgelines in some places, which break up and soften the countryside, whereas today the fields stretch away without as much as a bush to give the walker a bearing.

I first visited the Somme in 1986 and recall a very hot day on the 70th Anniversary of the battle's first day. Since then, many small but very interesting features found in subsequent visits have disappeared. That bit of old trench in an inaccessible corner of a field; a small crater that once provided the demarcation line between two fields. Much of this loss has been caused by the ridiculous rules governing the European Common Agricultural Policy that pays a higher subsidy to farmers if they can increase their hectares while, on the other hand, giving them generous incentives to do nothing with large tracts of land which we know as set-aside.

Some of this kind of activity can have alarming consequences, as with one example when a farmer decided to incorporate a small quarry which bordered his field for cultivation, only to unearth a large quantity of trench mortars known as 'toffee apples'. This would not normally be a problem for the bomb disposal unit, or *démineurs* as they translate into French, but these turned out to be filled with lethal gas instead of the usual high explosive. Apparently they were the result of an experiment to develop a high-speed gas delivery service that had to be abandoned!

Either the passage of time, or a failure by the current farmer to enquire of his elders as to the reason this ground had been left undisturbed, resulted in a very nasty situation which required the *démineurs* to transport their cargo to a remote part and detonate the lot, accompanied by the local television station's film crew. I was quite pleased that the wind was blowing in the direction of Amiens some twenty miles to the south of our house. The obvious lesson to be learned from this is that there is sometimes a very good reason why that little bit of ground has remained untouched by previous generations of farmers.

Heavy Artillery in action.

The Somme Battlefield remains today, as it always has been, one vast abandoned ammunition dump. True, there does not seem so much material about these days, especially hand grenades or the British eighteen pounders which were filled with lead balls and which were used in such profusion, but the ploughs that seem to get bigger all the time get down much deeper and much larger calibre munitions are being unearthed. On a ridge near Beaumont-Hamel on the exact site of the old German front line, large British shells have been appeared regularly in recent years after the ploughing. They are all unexploded and of the same calibre as shown in film the 'Battle of the Somme', which shows shells being hoisted into large guns situated in Mailly Maillet Wood. I have often wondered whether it was one of those guns in the wood, perhaps one of them actually being filmed, that was firing those 'blanks'. The farmer has to put rope around them to tow them to the side of the field. The largest shell I have ever seen was in the same location. Not being an expert on armaments, I have no idea what it was, but the farmer did not attempt to move it. Instead he put a rope fence around it, erected a red flag and no doubt, went off to make a telephone call. There is a similar calibre shell, defused, in the back of Thiepval church, possibly having some significance for the village. I put my arms around it but my hands could not be clasped together. I stand about 5 feet and 8 inches but it was taller than me, without its nose cone (fuse).

It is sometimes interesting to reflect that when news reports come through about an unexploded bomb having been found in the United Kingdom, it follows that the whole area is normally evacuated. Life in the Somme could not go on if that had to happen there. I remember parking my caravan on the site at Authuille years ago, before I took up residence here. The van was not level and I attempted to rectify this by digging under one wheel but with great difficulty because the wheel was resting directly on top of an unexploded British eighteen pounder!

So if you are nervous about all this, it is probably better not to come and visit the battlefields, although it is true to say I know of no casulaties to visitors here. One teacher did take home a grenade, though, in recent years. I read of his death in the British press as he had decided to 'fiddle' with it. There are casualties, all but a few caused by 'fiddling' so if you do not touch, you should be quite safe. The biggest danger to British visitors is to fail to remember to drive on the right hand side of the road. Please take note of the comments in 'Visiting the Battlefields'. The only accidents that I am aware of, that are truly accidental, are when farmers hit something with machinery and it explodes. This, thankfully, is now rare on the Somme, though more common in other parts, such as Verdun. The last incident I heard of was near Mailly Maillet over three years ago when a tractor was blown over by an unexploded shell. However, when the emergency services arrived, there was no sign of the driver. Local 'gossip' assured me he was eventually found at home, injured and very disorientated, but not so very badly that he had forgotten how good red wine is for you in these circumstances and of which he had a large glass on the table. He spent some days in hospital but clearly the wine had done the trick.

The Somme is also a large graveyard. I refer not only to the many military cemeteries, British, French and German, but also those of minority nationalities, such as Chinese and Indian. I am also thinking of the many soldiers who were never found and this as distinct from those who were buried without name. Someone once told me that there were about 200,000 British and Commonwealth soldiers wholly unaccounted for who, therefore, still lie undiscovered in the fields. Whether these figures are accurate I cannot be sure, but they serve to illustrate the point I am making that there are a great many men still left out here on the Somme, in spite of more regular finds of remains in recent years. It is not unusual for the visitor to the battlefields to come across human remains. These may not be substantial, perhaps a fragment of a finger or a tooth, although complete bodies are not uncommon. So if you are put off by this, then this is another reason why the Somme may not be for you.

The number of soldiers found in recent years does seem to have increased. There could be a number of reasons for this, among which I would include the most obvious: that there are more people visiting the Somme now than ever before. Couple more eyes looking, with bigger ploughs ploughing more land as arable farming takes over from dairy herds and beef, and this would seem a reasonable conclusion.

There is, though, a more sinister scenario. For many years, there has been a subculture among some locals for collecting war memorabilia, especially personal items, badges and equipment. I have seen items in personal collections which I have to conclude must have come from the discovery of a body. In one case, I saw several items including a name tag and a personal medallion and chain inscribed 'Leeds Pals'. The chances of finding just one of these items are not high. I checked the name and found that this was a young officer in the West Yorkshire Regiment, killed at Serre on 1 July and

A Royal Artillery cap badge is washed out by the rain.

never found, that is until a French 'collector' plundered his remains. His name is on the Thievpal Memorial, one of two sons lost to the Rector of Cleckheaton, where in the church there are two memorials.

Finding remains often involves the illegal use of metal detectors. First banned in the Département of the Somme, and later in the Pas de Calais, so the operators of these machines have to rebury the evidence for fear of being prosecuted. In the past a blind eye was turned quite often. I recall meeting an Englishman who told me he had been approached by two gendarmes in a bar. 'You 'ave a detector?' they asked him. 'No' he assured them repeatedly. They persisted 'Look, we know you 'ave a detector and we want to borrow it!' An encounter today with the gendarmes on this subject would not produce a similar outcome. Much has been done to clear the battlefields of the debris of war and also target those armed with detectors, whose ranks have been swollen by British prospectors in recent years. Be warned, an inability to speak French will not be regarded as immunity from prosecution, most of the forms at the Gendarmerie these days are printed in an English version.

A few years ago, some skeletons were reported in Flat Iron Copse. Supposedly the authorities had been alerted. A few days later they were still there and so I led the gendarmes to the spot myself after my daughter, Helen, and I had investigated. Of course, they had been stripped of everything and only their boots identified them as being British. What looked like two soldiers, turned out to be three. Later as I made a statement at the gendarmerie the officer turned to me and said, albeit with a little smile on his face, 'You should not go around digging up France'. The upsetting fact that he suspected me was tempered with the thought that at least they are taking these things seriously.

Later we visited the cemetery at Terlincthun near Boulogne and paid our respects. By coincidence they were buried next to a New Zealand soldier found previously at the White City just near our house. By contrast, he had not been robbed. He was intact with all his equipment, he came from Auckland, but his name tag, manufactured of fibre, had long since disappeared. Now all soldiers found on the battlefield are buried locally and the practice of taking them to Boulogne discontinued.

It is likely that the increased diligence being shown by the authorities is having an effect as the numbers of soldiers found and reported continues to rise. Previously energetic prospectors have by their own admission restricted, if not discontinued altogether, their activities, it is hoped, realising the error of their ways and that these soldiers of yesteryear are the grandfather, father, uncle or brother of someone still alive today who may have very real memories of him.

I have designed the walks so that those who may not wish to walk an extended distance all at once can make the journey in easy stages. Those who are of a more energetic nature can dovetail them together for a longer distance. The most obvious point to start from is the Ancre British Cemetery and park your car there. However, once in the cemetery or on your walk it is entirely hidden from sight and could fall prey to an opportunist thief. Because you are away from home enjoying the peace and solitude of the Somme, do not be mislead into thinking that this could not happen. In recent years, groups and individuals have targeted cars parked not only at cemeteries, but even at car parks at the major memorials. As with the metal detector brigade, the gendarmes have targeted this problem and seem to have had some success. Do not rely on this, however. If you have to leave some possessions in the car, leave them out of sight and never leave video cameras, money, credit cards, passports and such like. The Ancre British Cemetery has been one of the locations to suffer from this kind of crime, so even if you are away for only a few minutes, be on your guard. I know of one couple who went in for about five minutes and the deed had been done. All that said, on balance, it is not likely to happen.

Never park in a way that blocks agricultural or any other access. I often park my car up the track to the right hand side of the cemetery, far enough so it cannot be seen from the road, but leaving space for any farm vehicle to pass. Much will depend on the state of the ground, be careful not to get bogged down. There, you will at least be able to see your car while you visit the cemetery although not all the time if you set off on a walk. Alternatively, it is best to park in the village of Hamel, by the church is a good spot, and make the short walk to the cemetery.

Walk One

THE BRITISH FRONT LINE 1 JULY 1916
Attack of the 9/Royal Irish Fusiliers and 12/Royal Irish Rifles

The Ancre British Cemetery is situated between the two different British front lines from which the attacks described in this book were made.

Looking up towards the Cross of Sacrifice from the entrance, on the

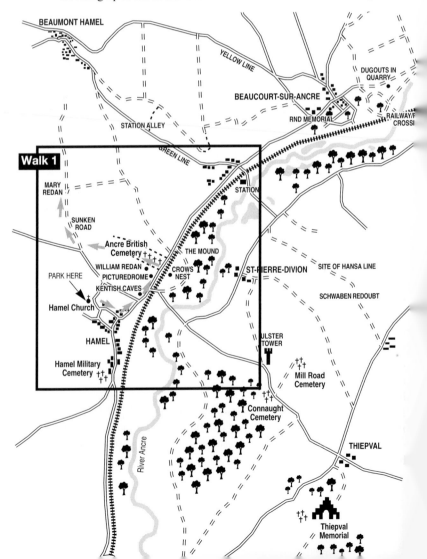

Snow capped headstones. Ancre British Cemetery.

left hand side you will see the steep bank which surprised the men of 36th (Ulster Division) by its depth and severity and today it remains an obstacle to the visitor hoping to make the journey in the opposite direction. Those with some agility and energy may be able to find a place, especially near the road where it is not so steep, but the easiest way to find your way to the old trench line from where the Ulstermen emerged to attack is to walk up the valley until the ground levels out and walk around the end of the bushes and retrace your footsteps along the top of the bank.

I cannot say there are many places on the Somme that I find oppressive or 'spooky', as some might say. One is Mametz Wood with its tales of Welsh voices calling out. This little valley, though, enclosing as it does all its dead within its folds, has always made me feel ill at ease. I cannot say why, except that it seems to want to wrap you up and keep you there as well, like the dead. Perhaps it is because you cannot see very far, unlike so many other places on the battlefields, and the thought that there might be someone watching you. Indeed one day there was. My wife and I together with our dog were walking down into the valley when suddenly a man stepped out from behind a bush. He had clearly been observing us for some time and he gave us quite a start. 'Is that your car?' he asked, and 'was that you walking on the ridge?' He eyed the dog suspiciously. 'Don't go into the copses,' he warned pointing across to the other side of the valley, 'There are traps in there!' I explained that I was English and writing a book, pushing my maps and notes under his nose. He was not impressed, but seeing I had no gun and was obviously not a poacher, he looked again at Kennedy (an Alsatian) whose hackles were now up, and disappeared into the bushes from where he had emerged.

On another occasion, I was walking up the valley with a friend and he was scuffing about under the bushes on the left hand side when, partially buried, he found a tank shell. It had not been fired but was without its brass shell case. This is quite close to the place as described in the battle narrative of 14 November where the tanks attacked the infamous strongpoint. Could this possibly be a remnant of that action? Probably not, but it would be nice wouldn't it?

To continue your walk, go along the top of the bank. Today, your view to the left, the direction of the attack, is largely obscured by the blackthorn and other undergrowth, especially in the summer months. This would have provided some cover for the attackers, but we do not know if it existed at that time. Perhaps it did, for it was from a position thirty yards to your right, somewhere along the top of this bank, that Captain Johnston of C Company 9/Royal Irish Fusiliers sent his runners back with the message that he was held up. This was not only because of machine-gun fire but because of the severity of the descent down the bank. As you are walking, look again to your right, the direction from which the Ulstermen came. If you check map 1 you will see that the British front line lay a varying distance of between 300 to about seventy-five yards at its narrowest point near the Hamel-Beaucourt road. Pity the poor runners as they retraced their steps over the bullet swept ground from whence they had recently come. Elsewhere in this book, I will mention an old friend of mine, Vic Simpson, who recounted to me tales of his exploits as a runner with the Duke of Wellington's Regiment but through it all never sustained even as much as a scratch. Well, just one of Captain Johnston's messengers survived this journey.

Whether you are able to get on to the old front line will depend on the time of year and whether there are any crops growing in the field which belongs to Jean-Paul Magny, the deputy mayor of Beaumont-Hamel. He is a friendly fellow and would not mind an exploration as long as nothing is growing in the field. The accuracy of your position will depend on how good you are at estimating distances, for there is nothing to give a bearing on, not even a bush. In my experience, people are notoriously inaccurate at these calculations, which are not easy. I myself usually resort to pacing it out. So if you are really intent on standing on the old front line, that is one way, if the conditions allow. The front line trenches from which the attack was made were called Sloane Street and Wateau Road.

The front line met the road, as mentioned, at the point closest to the Ancre British Cemetery, where it is possible today to stand on the point of a little salient known as the Picturedrome. The ground has not changed since the day of the attack on 1 July 1916. Situated as it is, high up on the bank by the side of the road, it is easy to see why it was

View from the Picturedrome.

named as such and compared to the new places of entertainment, where it was possible to see all kinds of moving pictures, except that the entertainment here was of a somewhat different nature. To stand here, then, and look across the shortest distance to the German front line on the opposite bank of the gully where, on the forward slope the hidden machine gun post that did so much damage to the men of the 36th Ulster Division was situated, was to invite certain death. If that was not enough, then look across to the right towards the village of St Pierre Divion and the slopes of the hill behind, in which where dug deep German trenches that prevented access to the even more impenetrable Schwaben Redoubt. It is not difficult to understand how exposed the Ulstermen were to considerable enfilade fire from this direction. It was from this position that Lieutenant Lemon set out to attack the tunnels and dugouts in the high bank along the Hamel-Beaucourt road. Many of his men were hit by fire from that machine gun. The survivors by-passed it by keeping to the road and were able to make progress, but at a price. A short walk along the road towards Beaucourt will bring you to the high bank on the left and, especially in the winter when the vegetation has fallen back, it is still possible to locate vestiges of these excavations.

The position where you are now standing was also known to the Ulstermen as William Redan and appeared on some of the maps at the time of the attack as such, but not all. I have not found a similar reference in the maps of the attacks made at a later date, so it is reasonable to assume that this was a name used by the Ulstermen. There is another point on this section of front line known as Mary Redan, which neatly makes the William and Mary connection with its

Irish connotation. William Redan marked the most southerly point, while Mary Redan the most northerly. Interestingly, though, the latter did appear on all the trench maps, and the name continued to be used in later battles.

See map
no. 2
page 28

Before leaving this position, note the piece of inaccessible raised ground across the other side of the railway line. This was known as the Crow's Nest, for obvious reasons, and could not have been a very sought after location. The main access to this important position was near the level crossing over the railway line by way of a trench called Moss Side, thence up a communication trench named the Devil's Staircase. Two forward saps, called Lancashire Post (confirming a previous northern occupation), would have been used not only for observation, but also as protection with at least some Lewis gun positions, as this was the point where the terrain became so marshy, adjacent to the river, that the British trenches terminated. It was from this position that the other half of Lieutenant Lemon's Company made their attack. The Germans, though, by contrast managed to extend their line a bit further around the area called the Mound before terminating their line. We shall return to that area later for a short diversionary walk but; meanwhile continue with a look at the more northerly end of 108 Brigade front line. As you retrace your steps, look into the gully, the site of the now peaceful Ancre British Cemetery and, in its place, try to imagine the scene of carnage and suffering that took place there on 1 July 1916: men caught up in the rolls of barbed wire which had been pushed down there by the Germans, the wounded being brought back behind the forward slope away from the frontal fire but only into the middle of the German barrage that had been laid directly into the gully. Look at Map 12 and locate the position of the hidden machine gun post [it is not easy because of the bushes] which continually swept the area and which alone was responsible for so many of the casualties. As this walk progresses, we will visit that machine gun position and this will be the most favourable position to appreciate its deadly role.

Continue on your walk up the left hand side of the valley, keeping to the rough ground or the edge of the fields. Here you are crossing the ground of the 12/Royal Irish Rifles C and D Companies (in that order) as they attacked from your left to the right. There is a small village in Northern Ireland called Bushmills which is famous, and rightly so, for its whisky. Many of its young men joined up and there seems to have been many of them in D Company of the 12/Royal Irish Rifles, which was led by Sir Harry MacNaghten, himself from a Bushmills family. This probably stems from the 'Pals' psychology of keeping men together to generate a sense of belonging and identity. As we know, this was to have devastating effects on local communities if a battalion suffered unduly and Bushmills, with a population of about 2,000, is a good example of this. On 1 July 1916, 23 men were killed and, by the end of the Battle of the Somme in November, a further ten had succumbed. By the end of the war a total of ninety-two were dead; included in this are nine sets of brothers. Bushmills men were awarded thirteen decorations: one Victoria Cross, two Military Crosses, seven Military Medals, two Distinguished Conduct Medals and one French Croix de Guerre.

As you approach a small tarmac road you are very close to the old front line on your left and almost exactly on it where you actually step onto the road. This trench was called Victoria Street, along with many others with obvious London connections in the immediate area, such as Buckingham Palace Avenue and Shooters Hill, through which some of the troops will have filed into the front line. The front line continued on up the side of the Hamel-Auchonvillers road for about 200 yards and it is possible to pick up the line by going round the front of a bit of scrubland to the left. Thereafter, it turned sharply to the right and continued across the field towards the site of Mary Redan. This was the position occupied by A Company. There is nothing to indicate along the side of the road that a trench once existed there. When the road was rebuilt later this probably obliterated all traces, although recently I investigated the efforts of a local farmer to boost his subsidy by ploughing a couple of furrows nearer the roadside quite near to the British front line at Beaumont Hamel and found lots of cartridges and cartridge cases, both French and British, and also a Lee Enfield .303 rifle almost entirely in a skeletal state but with its brass baseplate with the little hinged opening to receive the oil bottle and 'pull through' which still survived, complete with oil in the bottle. So you never know.

The metalled road is the same described as the 'sunken road' in the battalion diaries and the battle narrative. The men of the Royal Irish Rifles, A and D Companies, moved forward before zero hour on 1 July and sheltered in the road and under the bank that extends to the right. It should not be confused with its better known namesake near the Hawthorn Crater at Beaumont Hamel, filmed for posterity by Geoffrey Mallins on 1 July just before the attack, but it served a similar and no less useful purpose. Situated in No Man's Land under the comparative shelter of its shallow banks, it provided a little respite from the incessant machine gun-fire and an opportunity, as we have read, to regroup and reorganise. It is not difficult to picture that last little group of forty-six survivors huddled among their wounded, dying and dead comrades, being exhorted to greater effort, just before the whole thing was called off. Later the front line was established there.

Continue up the road and there is usually a very large manure heap on the right hand side with its attendant run off to negotiate. As the road levels off there is a track ahead that turns to the right. You are now standing on the site of Mary Redan, a curious little salient in the British front line. This was the dividing line between the 36th Division and the 29th Division and is also the most northerly point covered by this book. It was also the divisional boundary for the other actions described in the book, although the objectives were different.

Look towards the Newfoundland Memorial Park and you will see how close it is. Turn round and look towards the Thiepval Memorial and you will get some idea of the extent of the 36th Divisional front. Most people seem to associate the attack of the Ulster Division with Thiepval, but although the attack in that part of the front lies within the Commune of Thiepval, the attack on the village was made by the 32nd Division. Few realise that while approaching the end of their journey to visit the Park, they are still in territory stained with the blood of Ulstermen and that they are not far from the communal boundary with Auchonvillers. It is possible to appreciate while making this walk that the distance of about 600 yards, which was the approximate frontage of the attack by the 12/Royal Irish Rifles, would render the assault with only three companies very lightweight.

Do not get bogged down!

Walk Two

THE BRITISH FRONT LINE
Attack of 3 September and 13 November 1916

After the attack of 1 July, digging started immediately on a new forward trench system. This reduced the distance between the opposing front lines and avoided the necessity of negotiating the steep side of the gully by creating a position on the bank on the right-hand side, where there is now a copse. Whether the trees existed there in 1916 it is not possible to be sure, but I would think not. There are none shown on the trench maps and if there were, they would probably have been cut down as they would impede an advance. In all likelihood, there was just a bank, along the top of which ran the most forward position known as Gordon Trench and along the bottom of the bank was Roberts Trench. Unless dug by someone with those names, I assume they were named after our two well-known generals. The two trenches were linked at the southern end, that is near to the road, in a defensive flank, although saps extended from here and were very close to the German forward positions along the top of the bank by the road and that infamous machine gun position.

Both the September and the November attacks were made from this new position which was more favourable and avoided the long exposed

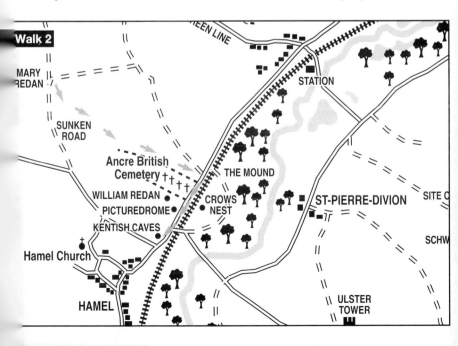

Looking down the line of the British Front from near Mary Redan, attacks of 3 September and 13 November.

approach and drop into the gully. Even so, the 39th Division proved another lightweight effort, as we have seen, and was easily repulsed by the Germans. After the battle, the reports that the Germans had been able to easily out range their attackers with their grenades and stick bombs was rejected at Corps Headquarters. What else could be expected for, although this was clearly true, this message could not be sent abroad for reasons of morale. If the men of 39th Division had been given a greater supply of bombs, this could have made a difference, as the Mills bomb was more powerful than their German counterparts.

I conducted my own experiment with two of the bombs mentioned; they had been defused, I hasten to add. First, I threw a British Mills bomb and then the German stick grenade. I repeated this three times and, each time, was able to propel the German product 20-25 yards further. While on the subject of Mills bombs, I met a young woman and her husband walking on the battlefields and it transpired her maiden name was Mills and that her great grandfather had invented the grenade of that name. I am told that approximately 50 million were used in the Great War, but he made no money out of this as he did not patent it. She did not posses an example of her great grandfather's ingenuity, but I was able to rectify that omission and I duly presented her with a good (defused) example, with which she was delighted.

The new line for the two attacks is easy to follow by walking round one side of the copse and returning round the other side of the copse. It continued northwards and straightened, running under the shelter of the bank and linking with the sunken road. Whether you venture into the copse is a matter for your own discretion. Although warned by the gamekeeper to beware of traps (*piége*), the only doubtful items I have seen are a few rusting unexploded shells. However, the man is not too friendly and I could be wrong about the traps, so be warned.

Drawing from the battle narratives of both 3 September and 13

November it is interesting to note that the strongest opposition, from the strongpoint opposite Mary Redan, and the machine guns at the redoubt on the right of the attack nearer the Hamel-Beaucourt road, was encountered from similar positions, as was also the case with the 1 July assault. Certainly the brigade reports written after the first attack, which pinpointed these positions, were available. Furthermore, the 39th Division's experience on 3 September when the 14/Hampshire attacked from the same position as the Hawke battalion and were annhiliated, might have provided some clues. Hindsight, of course, has considerable advantage.

Work on four tunnels which were driven forward towards the German front line started soon after 1 July. They were originally intended to enable small mines to be placed under the German lines. They were not completed in time for either the attack on 3 September or 13 November. The entry points of these tunnels are unknown.

The British front line at the southern end, known as William Redan, remained largely unaltered as it was overlooked by the Germans. No detailed accounts of operations have been found of 3 September attack in that area, but on 13 November the 1/Honourable Artillery Company went over from the Picturedrome and the Crow's Nest, the positions as described in Walk 1.

As already mentioned, Edmund Blunden, was in this area with his unit, 11/Royal Sussex, on 3 September. In his book, *Undertones of War*, he describes being in a position, behind the front line, called Kentish Caves. This place also crops up in a poem written by A P Herbert, who returned to this area after the war, and wrote *Beaucourt Revisited*. I have found no reference to it in any of the diaries or reports, but believe its location to be just forward of Hamel village, on

Looking up the British Front Line from William Redan.

Tangled undergrowth covers the remains of Kentish Caves.

the left as the railway crossing is approached. Whether it is possible to get right into the position will depend on whether there are any cattle in the field. There is an entrance to two fields, the one on the left is sometimes closed as cattle graze, but the one to the right is arable and, keeping to the left, it is still possible to get close. The position will be obvious, tucked in under the bank at the back. There is clear evidence of substantial chalk excavations and mounds of broken ground such as that created by shelling. On 1 July this place was only just behind the Ulster Division's front line and suggests that it may have been utilised then. On 3 September it was certainly in use and, recalling that A P Herbert was not in the initial battle on 13 November, but came forward later, could this be where he spent the first part of that conflict?

This supposition of this location is supported by an original trench map dated February 1916 (Map 1, used to illustrate the jumping off positions on 1 July) which shows the British trenches and marks a trench named Kentish Villas linking the second line to the location described above. In later maps this trench was renamed Foch Avenue.

Walk Three

THE GERMAN FRONT LINE

Back at Mary Redan we can now pick up the German positions. Turn right along the track already described. This more or less follows the divisional boundary with the 29th Division and would have been heading straight towards the German wire about 200 yards away. In the field on the right, was the site of a small salient that contained the strongpoint from where the machine guns that did so much damage to the Ulster battalions operated. Do not confuse this with the strongpoint further down the slope that caused the 14/Hampshire and the Hawke Battalion so much trouble.

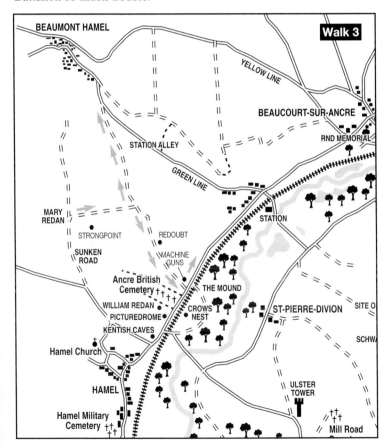

View across The Circus to Station road (Green line) and Station Trench on top of the banking.

There is nothing to see now except a depression in the ground, which could be a natural feature, and an area of chalk and flint which might be the remnants of its excavations. There does not even seem to be the usual clues to a previous utilisation: in some cases it is possible to see bits of broken bottles or rum jars, cartridge cases and traces of red brick which was one way of getting rid of the rubble of the smashed villages, by filling in the deeper trenches. It was here on 13 November that Lieutenant Cox and Lieutenant McMahon and their men of the 10/Royal Dublin Fusiliers captured the strongpoint by bombing the frontline entrances and knocking out the machine gun posts. Not far from here, too, Father Thornton negotiated the surrender of a German battalion. About another 100 yards down this track, also on the right and about 200 yards distant, is the approximate position of the attack on the German front line made by D Company 12/Royal Irish Rifles involving Sir Harry MacNaghten and the events described in Chapter One. It is reasonable to assume that this was roughly the area where Private Quigg searched for him and as a result was awarded the Victoria Cross. There is little else to see in the immediate area of interest, but the views here are very wide and far-reaching and the walking is easy as it is a gentle downhill gradient all the way. The village of Beaucourt can be seen and gives an appreciation of the distance of the 63rd Division's objective. The Thiepval Memorial stands out as too does the Ulster Tower. On a clear day, follow the line of pylons on the left and you may be able to see High Wood and Delville Wood, as they pass close by to both. When you reach the junction of another track you will have passed over the German second line and be standing on their third position. Here there is an option either to turn right and follow the track down back to the Ancre British Cemetery or take a short detour to the left. A short walk will bring you to a re-entrant on the right along which, on each bank, are the remains

Looking from the site of Mary Redan down the track to the German frontline. The Redoubt captured by the Dublins was in the field to the right.

of some excavations, this position was known as the 'Circus'. The excavations are very regular and suggest the possible site of dugouts and entry points through which the Germans could enter and exit their defensive positions via an underground route. Their proximity to the third line and the communication trenches marked on the map running forward, where you are now standing, could point to this. It is said that the whole ridge was linked between Y Ravine, the end of which is a bit further down the track towards Beaumont and the tunnel entrances in the Hamel-Beaucourt road. Unfortunately this small pasture you are looking at is the last remaining in Station Road. I remember when more of these little fields showed similar evidence, but the plough has since erased it. Over to the left you will see the large chalk quarries which look almost exactly as they did in 1916. They were not in the 36th Division's sector but the extreme right hand end fell into the 63rd Division's remit. Anyway it is worth recounting that about 10 years ago an opening appeared, probably an old airshaft uncovered by recent

Ground plan of tunnels in Quarries.

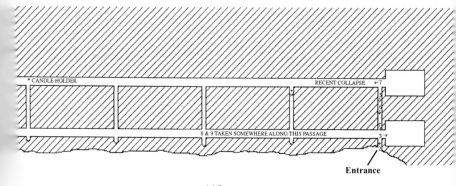

* CANDLE HOLDER   RECENT COLLAPSE ←7

8 & 9 TAKEN SOMEWHERE ALONG THIS PASSAGE

Entrance

Beaumont Quarries, then and now. Note the ventilation shafts in the original

SITE OF ENTRANC

In the tunnels near the entrance

quarrying activity. It was possible to slide down this shaft as it was not vertical and about 30 feet down arrive in a network of tunnels of Teutonic construction. They were clearly so, as no other people would take such care to cut the chalk so accurately and with such precision! As you can see from the plan, everything was measured and symmetrical. I joined in the activities of those interested enough to take a look, just once, and slid down the hole with some trepidation which increased to some magnitude when I realised that much of the 'ceilings' consisted of large boulders of chalk which just seemed to be hanging there defying gravity while others had abandoned this trick of levitation and fallen, crushing the now rotten timber supports as they did so. There was nothing of interest except the rusting candle holders and their niches cut into the chalk and the black stains made by the candle smoke. Evidently, this part of the German underground system had yet to benefit from electrification or perhaps they had had a lot of power cuts! I did not stay long but I am indebted to my friend Sean Joyce for his detailed survey and photographs reproduced here. Soon afterwards, the Mayor of Beaumont, Monsieur Omiel, curtailed any further activity by having the shaft blocked up and rightly so! The hole is still very obvious and hopeful explorers still have a look to see if there has been any further movement, but the mayor seems to have won the day.

We return to the junction of the two tracks and continue along the ridge. The German second line ran along the right hand edge of the track for a short distance and where it crossed the track, joined up with the front line. In the field on the right, the German third line contained two more large redoubts that commanded that area and prevented capture of that position. It was not until the tanks captured the redoubt that the occupants of these two positions capitulated and raised the white flag too. Thereafter, the front and second lines separated again and ran along the left hand side of the field. You are now walking back into No Man's Land.

From this position it is very easy to appreciate the task confronting attackers who had managed to penetrate this far. It was an uphill slog without a scrap of cover and total exposure to fire from every direction, with the possible exception of the rear, including that of the massive Schwaben Redoubt on the other side of the valley. Another walk will take you to that position and will facilitate views which, at certain times of the year, will show the German trench lines clearly defined in the fields to your left, by the white chalk subsoil dug out, but not ploughed back in, even after all these years. Near the point where the

A tunnel opens up on the site of the Redoubt.

German front line crosses the track, if you look carefully in the bank on the left hand side, you will see what at first appears to be a small 'pill box'. If it is summer, it is very overgrown but quite obvious in the winter. My first opinion that it would have had some kind of entrance from below, was challenged when I saw it again without its vegetation and realised it had no upper openings (i.e.windows), neither could I be sure that it had any foundations. I came to the later conclusion that this large rectangular object is a remnant of one of the strongpoints in the area, perhaps the one attacked by the tanks during the assault by the 63rd Division. If so, a good job was made of moving it. Today's machinery could do it easily but horsepower (quite literally) was the most common form of energy used in the1920s, and it was put there as neatly and tidily as if the Germans had done it themselves!

The site of the infamous redoubt is a little further down the track in the field on the left. Here the attackers fell in large numbers and Captain Montague witnessed the carnage when he returned to the area after the battle. The tanks rumbled down the valley on your right and turning left attempted to get up the slope to your right. All this was preceded some months before by the struggles of the brave Ulstermen and the efforts of the other winner of the Victoria Cross that day in July, Lieutenant Cather. These are obvious and only token examples of all the gallantry and sacrifice that occurred here in this pathetically small area as you complete your walk down the track through No Man's Land, the larger proportion of which would now be to your right as the German front line was close by in the field on your left.

Once again there is nothing to see of the redoubt. It was all underground and completely disguised to look like a communication trench from the air. It had several machine gun positions and a fuller description of its construction has already been given. No doubt its remains still exist deep under the fields. From time to time, holes open up in these fields as, somewhere much deeper down, another tunnel collapses or a tractor lurches uncontrollably as its weight proves too

The road from Hamel to Beaucourt, site of Railway Sap, where Lieutenant Archie Lemon climbed the bank to bomb the machine gun posts and dugouts in the embankment. (See page 28)

much for the fragile ground below. The redoubt is still, even today, a danger to the unwary.

As you descend the final few yards on the track, walk up into the field on your left and onto the bank high up alongside the road. About fifty yards further on, the German front line met the road, but a sap continued at a right angle along the top of the bank directly towards the position where you are standing. Within a few yards of this point there was the concealed machine gun position which took its due toll, especially on 1 July. It is easy to see the field of fire, the operators enjoyed with almost unobstructed views up the gully and the fate of any men attempting to get forward. (See photograph on page 28)

The trench crossed the road in the direction of the Mound and behind the wire here on the side of the road were several tunnels dug deep into the bank. These gave access to the strongpoint and the rest of the German trench system, even possibly as far as Y Ravine, as suggested. This was the position attacked by 12/Royal Irish Rifles No 8 Platoon and along the top of the bank is where Lieutenant Lemon climbed up and dropped grenades down openings into the tunnels below before being killed. As his party below had got behind the German front line, Lieutenant Lemon would have been some way behind the concealed machine gun position along the top of the bank. The 1/HAC were also here and were assisted in their progress along the top of the bank by the Lewis gun of the 14/Worcesters in the valley on your right.

Today, be careful on top of the steep bank. In the winter when the undergrowth is reduced I have observed the remains of large holes which could be dangerous. It is better to explore along the side of the road where, in winter particularly, it is possible to locate large

On top of the embankment looking at the Mound across the railway line. From there the HAC cleared the German trench and the Worcesters' machine guns fired across to the embankment. Also the position attacked attacked on 1 July by 12/RIF (see page 28).

depressions in the bank and other signs that tunnels existed there.

At this stage it is worth briefly considering the role and effect of the tanks, as we are near one of the positions where they came into the action. The other, it will be recalled, was on the other side of the river with the 39th Division on the same day, 14 November, and we will visit the site of that action too.

It is difficult to know what effect they had on the morale of the troops on the ground, but certainly the press were mostly enthusiastic, even if a little jounalistic licence and inaccuracies added a bit of spice to the reports. *The Times*, though, reported the events most accurately and this concurs with the Official History written some twenty-two years later.

> *...north of the river a tank was of material assistance in helping to clear the German first line trench.*

This seems to be the one driven by Lieutenant Commander Campbell. It also went on to describe the action of the 39 Division, south of the River Ancre:

> *One went forward and got ahead of our infantry into a position which was very strongly held by the Germans, who swarmed about it and tried to blow it up with bombs. It stood them off until our infantry came up and was very helpful in helping to clear out this wasps nest.*

Other reports, though, sound more like excerpts from *Ripping Yarns* and named the tank as *Devils Delight*.

The Huns rushed upon it, yelling like pawnees, improvising a scalp dance around the monster. Fearless and unruffled the tank closed its portholes and with drawn curtains and closed doors philosophically awaited the end of the shower. Occasionally it emitted a few cracking streams of bullets just to kill time, and also some Huns. Grenades slipped over its outer shell like lozenges on a whales back...shortly afterwards a solid detachment of British bombers advanced to the rescue and delivered the tank, which directed its nozzle towards the enemy.

Another account stated that the attack on the

> *...landcrab, lasted two hours, but it showed to the Germans only its toad complexioned carapace of inviolate steel and the spit of its guns.*

Yet another version not only stretches the imagination but fuses the two occasions on the same day, when tanks were used either side of the river, into one event the day after they actually took place.

> *Delices du Diable did marvellously well at Beaucourt, plunging forward like a huge elephant, he daringly dashed ahead of the waves of assault, and took up a position at the entry to the ruined village. At first the Germans took to their heels. Then back they came one by one. Machine guns, grenades, rifles and mortars tried to bore holes through his double carcass, but all in vain. Sitting well down on his haunches the majestic tank lorded it like Father Neptune. He courteously allowed himself to be approached. Some sappers tried to place bombs under him to blow him up. The crew inside laid low. The Germans grew bolder.*

A British tank is attacked by a flame thrower.

Then ten, twenty, thirty soldiers armed with lifting jacks and mallets tried to upset him. But what could even two battalions do against this amiable masterdom? The Colonel, mad with rage, fired eight shots with his revolver at close range. If he could have laughed the tank would have burst with glee, but his joking is of a more military sort. Believing the crew annihillated and the monster disabled, at the end of a long quarter of an hour's silence, the Germans closely surrounded him. They were in large numbers. All of a sudden the portholes opened, machine guns spat fire from both sides, and the terrible beast crushed, flattened, riddled, slew, a real giant in action, grinding the dead under his feet. An hour later when the main body of British troops were able to reach Beaucourt, they discovered round the stranded tank dead, lying in heaps and wounded writhing in agony.

The tank speaks little, but to the point. Three cheers for Delices du Diable.

Well, what actually happened has been recorded, but tales of British daring and German incompetence, might have stirred the imagination back home, though the reality, it is safe to say, was not as uplifting for the men there at the time.

The tanks that came from Auchonvillers were probably kept in Auchonvillers Wood. Here, large pits had been dug, thirty-two feet long, sixteen feet wide and six feet deep, to accommodate and camouflage these vehicles. Today, some of the remains of these pits can be seen, but access is very difficult, especially in the summer months. The wood is little more than a copse but is privately owned and care should be exercised before any attempt to enter is made. There are signs of traps (*piége*) being set.

Walk Four

THE GREEN LINE

The most appropriate place to start this walk would be Beaucourt Station and there is a convenient place to park your car within the confines of the old station, which is now closed. The railway line that passes through used to be the important link between Lille and Paris. However, with the advent of the new high speed train (TGV) this line was downgraded a few years ago and carries mainly freight, a luxury, no doubt, rail chiefs in the United Kingdom wish they could afford. There are still some local passenger trains and one or two old style SNCF express services. When Beaucourt station was proposed for closure, a typically Gallic and amusing notice was posted which stated that 'Trains may or may not stop at this station in future'.

Your car should not attract attention here and there are people about, not least those patronising Medhi's Bar opposite, along with local

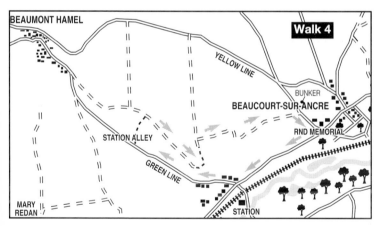

A French express passes through Beaucourt Hamel station, 2001.

houses and a small metalworking factory. Walk along the road signposted to Beaumont and on your left you will soon see the banking over which those who, at various stages of the battle, advanced towards the Green Line. This was known as Station Road. On the left bank, it is possible to discern traces of disturbed ground and this area was known as the 'Terraces'. Unfortunately recent ploughing has obliterated more substantial evidence of this and also of the 'broken' ground in the small fields at the side of the road which used to show evidence of the shelling it received first from the British artillery and, after it was captured, by the Germans. One by-product of this ploughing is the emergence of numerous shrapnel balls which can now be found, more especially the British lead variety. The Germans used steel balls and these have largely corroded away. Locals can often be seen filling their supermarket carrier bags and the local scrap dealers will give a few Euros as a reward for the British lead, which in turn will buy a few bottles of wine!

In the fields on the left there was a German trench which ran parallel to the road and was, in effect, the German fourth line. On top of the banking on the right was the position known as the Green Line, also running parallel to the road. Depending on which document or book consulted both these trenches were known as Station Trench. The Official Historian favours the German fourth line position on the left, while most battle maps of the time give the same name to the Green Line, which was the first main objective.

Walk on until you reach a small re-entrant on the right which leads directly up the bank. This was the site of Station Alley and it provides an opportune access to the top of the bank from where good views of the battlefield in both directions can be obtained. Look back into the valley below towards the Station, which is very close to the position where Commander Gilliland arrived after breaking through and where he waited for support before pushing on to the Yellow Line alone with his men. Nearer the position where you are standing was the point where the men of the Nelson Battalion arrived before moving on

Station Road (Green Line) and Station Alley Trench, 2001.

towards the Yellow Line and joining up with Commander Gilliland. Station Alley was the furthest point along Station Road that was held by the 63rd Division overnight on 13/14 November. Beyond here, there was a gap in the line before the village of Beaumont was reached, but it is not clear whether any German troops occupied it. If they did their position would have been precarious.

The valley of Station Road provided the overnight assembly position for most of the battalions who were to make the attacks on the morning of 14 November. The 13/King's Royal Rifle Corps had already passed through this point and advanced towards the Yellow Line, the Beaucourt-Beaumont road which is in the distance behind you, to link with Colonel Freyberg's left. The remaining battalions of 111 Brigade, the 13/Rifle Brigade and the 13/Royal Fusiliers together with those men of the 1/Honourable Artillery Company not already with Lieutenant Colonel Freyberg and the remnants of the 7/Royal Fusiliers, sheltered here overnight. There were also representatives of many other battalions of the Royal Naval Division, some of whom, as we have seen, arrived in the early hours of 14 November. Continue by turning right along the top of the bank back towards the station. Here there is a choice, where the track ends, to scramble down the bank and return to your car or to turn left and cut through for about 150 yards between the boundary of two fields and pick up a track that will take you across the ground occupied by the 13/King's Royal Rifle Corps and to the village of Beaucourt. As you do that, look across to the half left and towards the position of Munich and Frankfurt Trenches beyond the Beaumont-Beaucourt road. They were on the divisional boundary of the 51st Division and the attack by the battalions of 111 Brigade. The 13/Rifle Brigade and the 13/Royal Fusiliers attack in that direction was met with determined defence and they failed to get to the Yellow Line. The Germans realised that a successful attack there would considerably threaten the Munich and Frankfurt position which was an

At the top of Station Alley looking back over the ridge from where the RND came. The chalk marks are on the German third line.

important axis and had so far held out against the attempts of the 51st Division to take it.

When the next track has been reached, continue towards the village on the metalled road and cross the ground attacked by Captain Stock's D Company, the 13 King's Royal Rifle Corps, while on the left was Lieutenant Hawkins' C Company. He linked further on the right with Freyberg's mixed force. It is not possible to be absolutely sure of the exact positions of the troops, but a close study of the ground and some reasonably obvious deductions can give us a probable scenario. On Freyberg's right, the ground falls very steeply away from the road and is a sheer cliff of up to about 100 feet into what was then a bog. Anyone attempting to descend would also be fully exposed to snipers and machine-gun fire as well as the natural hazards. A map in the Official History gives Freyberg's right as resting on the railway line, a short distance from the cliff, but it is very small scale and therefore can only be approximate. Even today, as this walk unfolds it is possible to see that the ground is so wet that troops would have had difficulty negotiating it. I favour Freyberg's position as being the top of the cliff, rather than the railway line.

As you walk on the road towards the village look to the left and growing crops permitting, you will see a house and an adjoining barn on the Beaucourt-Hamel road which is about 150 yards from the Royal Naval Division Memorial and therefore coincides with the position from where Freyberg attacked the village. As you draw level with these (See map 10, page 85) buildings, you can imagine the troops dug in on your right and extending across to your left. Once again, it is not possible to be certain as to the position of Freyberg's left and the 13/King's Royal Rifle Corps right, but considering the number of troops at his disposal and the density required for a frontal attack on the village it must have been in the field on your right to the left of Engine Trench [see map on page 85]. We know that Captain Stocks advanced in the direction of the village following a communication trench towards a machine gun position, but he did not name it. There were two communication trenches that it could have been, on the left Redoubt Alley and further to the right Railway Alley. However, a glance at the map again, shows the 13/King's Royal Rifle Corps left resting on Redoubt Alley, and we know Captain Stocks advanced half right towards Beaucourt village which leaves Railway Alley as the most likely route.

All this would neatly fit the foregoing into a feasible disposition for the attack on the village. As you near the end of the road at a junction, you pass over the site of Railway Alley and a bit of simple orienteering shows that it led to the vicinity of a large German concrete bunker, which you can see by turning left and walking a short distance and looking into the corner of a small croft on the right. Was this the machine gun position one captured by Captain Stocks'men of the 13/ Kings Royal Rifle Corps?

If a longer walk is desired, it is possible to continue to the left and connect with the Beaucourt-Beaumont Road which, of course, is the continuation of the Yellow Line. Otherwise, turn round and walk down the hill. Further down the hill as the Beaucourt-Miraumont road is reached the Memorial to the 63rd Royal Naval Division will be found on the right hand corner. The old veteran friend of mine, Vic Simpson, told me of the time he spent later in Beaucourt with the Duke of Wellington's Regiment. He had to deliver a message to battalion headquarters and entered the village via Engine Trench, which ran parallel to the road in the field where the memorial is now situated. He eventually joined the road going in the direction of Miraumont and kept going. Suddenly he was challenged, 'And where do you think you're going?' a sentry demanded. 'Battalion headquarters', Vic replied. 'Well you won't find it down there' the sentry said, 'only Germans!'. Vic had been about to walk straight into the German front line. He found the headquarters which was in a quarry on the left as he went back. It was an old German dugout but as such faced the wrong way and the entrance was covered with a thick blanket so that at night no light would show and give the position away. Every time someone entered, a chorus of voices bellowed, 'Watch the bloody blanket!' I looked for the site of this dugout several times, but was unable to find

German machine gun post on the edge of Beaucourt.

Vic Simpson's quarry where, on the left, the captors of Beaucourt took over German dugouts.

Private A V Simpson, Duke of Wellington's Regiment.

any trace of a quarry. I found it, after all, very nearly where Vic had described it while exploring the ground in detail for this book.

Follow the road out of Beaucourt towards Miraumont and the road bridges a gully which only runs after heavy rain. The road dips to the right and then ascends and turns back to the left. At the top of the bank on the right, there is a very wide grass verge and a fence. Follow the fence along for a short distance and you will soon be looking down over the site and the obvious vestiges on the right of what Vic remembered all those years ago. Whether this position was established by the Royal Naval Division, we cannot be sure, but it would seem to be near the initial Red Line position, so Freyberg's men could well have been the original tenants.

If you wish to locate the final British positions on the Red Line by 19 November walk towards Miraumont for a short distance until a metalled track leads off to the left. This was where the line crossed the road and, on the left, it went up the field and passed to the right of the copse known as the Bois d'Holland and then turned left, following the shape of the wood. On the right, it ran down to the river bank then followed the river back towards the village, so forming a natural defensive position as far as the railway bridge over the river. A very pleasant walk can be had by proceeding up the metalled road, passing the copse on the right, in which there are still a few shell holes, and along the track. You are now in No Man's Land and walking towards Artillery Lane. Turn left at the second track and walk down to the metalled road that runs from Beaucourt to Puisieux. Turn left back towards Beaucourt and on the left some quarries will be reached. This

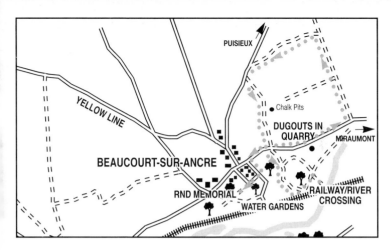

position was known as the Chalk Pits and features in an excellent book, *A Sergeant Major's War*, the story of Ernest Sheppard, who was eventually killed here when attacking with the 1/Dorset Regiment early in 1917. The quarries were fortified by the Germans and I have seen evidence of tunnels collapsing. A few years ago the road was improved to overcome flooding and a great deal of ordinance was unearthed which was left in the quarry for a very long time. Eventually, I noticed that someone had unscrewed the complete nose cone off the largest shell! They must have used a great deal of WD 40 and were probably lucky to escape with their lives. The whole little valley is very quiet and attractive and in the banks on the far side, some evidence of excavations can be seen on the site of Suvla Trench. Walk back towards the village, but

Entrance to a dugout at the Chalk Pits near Beaucourt.

The extreme right of the RND line was, at this picturesque spot, where the railway crosses the River Ancre.

leave the road where there is a track that forks to the left, it is a bit overgrown at first, so you may need to skirt round the edge of the field before rejoining the track which will bring you out near to the bridge over the gully.

To visit the right flank position where the railway line crosses the river, continue across the road and down the pleasant track that bears to the right. Turn left and continue about 250 yards towards some fishermen's caravans and you are in the area where the Royal Naval Division consolidated their right flank. The actual site of the railway bridge is reached by turning first right and walking a short distance. It was while returning from here that I spotted Vic's quarry which can be seen in the field half right/ahead, as it is not visible from the Beaucourt-Miraumont road.

Another pleasant detour can be made by returning the way you have come and turning left when the road is reached and then first left again. Continue on this road, which becomes a track, and it will lead you past some water gardens on the left and, on the right, to a most attractive small lake fed by a natural spring of the clearest water. If you continue it is possible to see the very high banks or cliff, as described, on the right, on which some of the village houses are perched and you will be able to make your own mind up as to whether Freyberg would have been able to deploy any of his forces in the valley bottom. It is an easy walk back through the village and past the Memorial to Beaucourt Station, but

Dedication of the RND Memorial and the Memorial today.

there is no pedestrian footpath so take care and remember that French cars tend to travel faster and always in the opposite direction to that in the United Kingdom.

From the trench maps of the day it is possible to see that the Memorial now stands on the site of the Yellow Line, the second objective, where it entered the village. This, it will be recalled, is the point reached by Freyberg, but from which he had to retire. Pace out 150 decent strides as you continue and you will be somewhere near the line where he dug in and waited, attacking the German provisions store in the meantime! I have measured this to be near the first house and barn on the left. It was from a line here and in the field up on the right (facing Beaucourt Station direction), that the final assault was made on the morning of 14 November by Freyberg's troops.

The Mound

As already mentioned, this position presents a curious little riddle in as much as the area so described could not be less of a mound by any exaggeration. Across the railway line, the ground here was, and still is, totally flat except for a slight rise towards the railway line. On the original coloured trench maps the area is clearly defined as a lake, the same blue as other lakes shown. On monochrome maps produced at divisional or battalion level, the outline of the lake could be mistaken for a contour line and so I lean towards the theory that this is how it was so named. On the other hand, it could be that some cynic named it thus, simply because it couldn't be any flatter! To have a look round the area will not take long and you will see immediately that there is no lake. If there was ever one there, what was it filled in with? Perhaps

View of the Picturedrome taken from the Crow's Nest. William Redan was near the entrance to the cemetery.

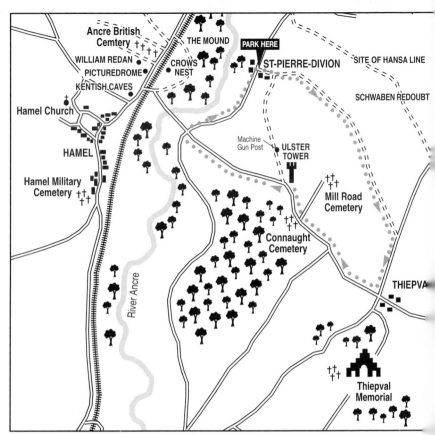

Map 15. Walk south of the River Ancre.

there is a large quantity of war debris under the present site. It is possible to get a closer look at the Crow's Nest and walk along the track and find the point where the German line terminated on the right hand side of the track as it curved to the left towards the railway line, at which point it cut through and across the road. It used to be possible to drive through here and as far as Beaucourt Station but the track is now gated. A walk, though, will enable you to explore the area which is full of fishing lakes, man made and dug out, as the water table is very high. All are privately owned, so care should be exercised. Some years ago, a Frenchman gave me a relic German Luger pistol he had found in this area.

St Pierre Divion

Across the River Ancre, there is another interesting diversion. After the railway level crossing and the river bridge, turn left at the bottom of the hill. This is the road along which the 16/Sherwood Foresters attacked on 13 November. Pass the chalet bungalow on the right and stop where there appears to be a natural opening on the bank on the right. There is a bit of a fence and an old gate. A few years ago this appeared to be an old quarry and it was possible to drive in and park up off the road. Some scratching about could easily locate spent cartridges, both British and German, and also some live SAA of both types. An indent in the back of the 'quarry' showed some ground movement and judging by the state of the chalk, I was not the only one to have shown interest, which showed disturbance. Sometime later I returned to have another look, but the scene had changed. The quarry had all but disappeared, filled in with soil and seeded. A fence had been erected and a padlocked gate barred the way. Why would anyone go to so much trouble and expense, if it where not to 'hide' something? We have seen that both in the village and tucked under the high bank here were many German dugouts and tunnels. There were also reported to be entrances to the Schwaben Redoubt and I am convinced that a large one of these lies not far below the topsoil here. The steep bank further down the lane was where troops of the Sherwood Foresters in the November attack trapped many Germans in these dugouts and tunnels. They threw phosphorous bombs (P. bombs) into them before entombing their opponents by blowing in the entrances. For some, there were alternative means of escape through to the village and the Schwaben Redoubt, although any able to make progress in that direction found British troops in occupation by then, hence the large number of prisoners taken.

A good account of these excavations written after the war described them thus:

Distant view of the Ulster Memorial Tower from Hamel Church. The chalk lines in the field mark the site of the German front line. The 49 Division attack on 3 September started from between the edge of the wood and the 'bloody road'; the 39 Division on 13 November from the area in front of the Tower. (See map page 43).

A captured German dugout with its boarded walls and ceiling, with spacious rooms leading off from the passages.

A very marvellous system of underground defences had been constructed in the steep clay bank on the riverside of St Pierre Divion. The bank was about twenty feet in height, with trenches along the top of it, but underneath a vast subterranean gallery had been excavated, four feet in width and eight feet high, its sides boarded and the whole thing lit by electric light. This gallery went back under the hillside for three hundred yards and then branched away at right angles to the right and the left making its ground plan roughly the shape of a gigantic T.

We called it the 'Tunnel,' and immense ingenuity had been displayed in its construction. Not only were there innumerable dugouts leading off the main passage, fitted with bunks and wooden walls, some of them papered, but also shafts, passing upwards to the heights above, through which the lurking garrison could ascend or retire as the case may be by solid wooden staircases of great breadth.

The success of the attack here can partially be attributed to the depth and comfort of these quarters. The onset of winter conditions had encouraged the Germans to take advantage of their billets and all their machine guns were down there with them. There is no doubt that the Germans were not expecting an attack at this time and many were asleep in their comfortable bunks when the Sherwood Foresters rushed through in the mist and darkness. Perhaps they had also been lulled into a sense of false security by the ease with which they had repelled previous attacks. There was no time to get the machine guns up together and working.

In the deeper recesses of this position the captors found immense

German soldier keeps watch in a snow covered trench.

quantities of stores of every description. There were machine guns and ammunition, and, it was alleged, explosive bullets; one of these was fitted in the machine gun belts to every twenty normal rounds. It was claimed, that they were only used to attack aeroplanes. The unpleasant smell was attributed to the baking of German bread which was also stored in great quantities!

There was an interesting consequence of the success of this attack. The Duke of Saxe-Coburg-Gotha was better known as the Duke of Albany, and nephew of King Edward VII. He was colonel in chief of some of the German regiments of the 38th Division at St Pierre Divion and had made a special journey to conduct a morale boosting inspection. The fresh troops of the 223rd Division were already on the way to relieve his men but were caught in a British barrage and took heavy casualties. They were unable to relieve the garrison, who were either all killed or taken prisoner, so the Duke had a wasted journey. (The Seaforth Highlanders were known as the Duke of Albany's.) It was later in 1917 that the Royal Family in the United Kingdom changed their name from Saxe-Coburg-Gotha to Windsor. To be fair to the Germans, the whole of the 38 Division was on the point of being relieved when the attacks of 13 November were mounted, on both sides of the river.

Walk on towards the little church. On the left, deep into the marshy ground near the river, but out of our view today, was the position known as the 'Summer House'. This was fortified as a machine gun post and somehow built on the swampy ground. It was probably positioned to defend the approach up the valley, where it was not possible to dig trenches, in case anyone was tempted to make an attack there. Turn left by the church. Here, there is a choice. You can either turn left again and return along the top of the bank behind the village. Here you will be on the site of the German trench called Mill Trench. Alternatively, there are two tracks. The one that goes straight on will take you to the site of the Schwaben Redoubt. Before reaching that, on the right as you climb the hill, quite close to the track that you are following, is the site of the Strasburg Line. German prisoners revealed that it was still over five feet in depth and had many dugouts. As the crest of the ridge is approached, the western edge of the Schwaben Redoubt is reached. This actually bordered onto the track onto which had been constructed four massive machine gun positions connected directly to the redoubt. Pass behind the Ulster Tower and Mill Road Cemetery as far as the Thiepval Communal Cemetery, where you should turn right. The landscape is bare, but I once took a friend to the approximate spot where his grandfather was killed attacking the redoubt. All he wanted was to find a little souvenir of his visit, perhaps a bit of shell fragment. Well, we found quite a few cartridges and were about to leave when I looked down and at his feet, there were some German tunic buttons with the Kaiser's Crown on them! It was in this area that Edmund Blunden set out on his foray deep into enemy territory, as described in his book, *Undertones of War*. His unit, 11 Royal Sussex, who were in support, were called forward to assist in clearing the dugouts, mainly in the Strasburg line, and as darkness fell, he completely lost direction.

Continue to the crossroads in the village and turn right again. On the way back you may wish to visit Connaught Cemetery, Mill Road Cemetery, and the Ulster Tower. The track that emerges coming up the hill to the Tower is the alternative and shorter route from St Pierre Divion Church. About a further 100 yards further down that track, on the right, is a good example of a German machine gun post. This is situated on the approximate site of the Pope's Nose and from here there are excellent long range and elevated views of the battlefield north of the Ancre and the Ancre British Cemetery. A further 100 yards on, also just on the right of the track, is where the tank, (*Delices du Diable*) fell through the dugout in the German second line and the fight to save the crew ensued. If you are visiting at a time when there are no crops in the fields it may be possible to see the long chalk marks in the fields sloping away from the Ancre British Cemetery on the right, the German positions, and also in the field on the left which denote the British trench lines of 1 July. Notice how easy it would have been for the German gunners to enfilade the British troops attacking on the north bank, even at this distance (see photograph on page 23). The return to St Pierre Divion can be made via the metalled road which was named the 'Bloody Road' as on both 1 July and 3 September it provided temporary respite for those trapped in No Man's Land. However, German shells soon made it untenable. On 3 September the Yorkshiremen pushed their front line forward almost to the edge of the road on the right to foreshorten the distance of the attack, but to no avail. On 1 July, further down the road, there was no assault at the St Pierre Divion end, which probably resulted in those defenders being able to concentrate on the Ulstermen across the river.

The Hansa Line

The rapid success of the 39th Division is all the more remarkable since, although part of the Schwaben Redoubt had fallen, the Strasburg Line was still holding out and, well beyond that, the formidable Hansa Line, which wrapped round its assailants like a snake, was over half a mile away over open country.

There is little to be seen, but an appreciation of the distance and terrain can be had by a pleasant walk up a track which is quite close to the trench. Park your car at Beaucourt Station and turn right over the railway crossing. Continue over the river bridge. This is the point where Lieutenant Colonel Freyberg and his men met up with the 1/1 Cambridgeshire and were resupplied. Continue to the road junction and turn right after a few yards, on the left, there is a track leading up to the ridge and ultimately the Thiepval-Miraumont road. The Hansa Line commenced behind the farm which you pass at the start of the walk and, as the walk progresses, comes gradually closer to the track the further you go. Exactly where the track makes a half turn to the right is where the trench crossed the track and continued into the field on the right following the contour of the ridge and on to connect with the rear of the Schwaben Redoubt, a further half a mile away. There is little option but to retrace your steps, but note the field of fire obtained from this position, especially on the left as you look back in the direction you have come from. The strongpoint was situated about 500 yards further down the road on the right, near to the poultry farm on the edge of Grandcourt village.

The site of the mill captured by the 1/1 Cambridgeshire is situated on private land to your left and is inaccessible. As far as I know there is nothing of the mill remaining.

Chapter Eleven

THERE IS A GREEN HILL FAR AWAY

A school has existed in Durham since Saxon times when the monks of the great Benedictine Monastery passed on the benefits of their own education. Until more recent years it was thought that the current school owed its lineage to those early days, but the evidence is not now thought conclusive of any direct descent before 1414. In 1539, Henry VIII dissolved the monastery at Durham and in 1541 it was re-founded as a cathedral and the school was reconstituted.

In 1844 the school removed from the environs of the cathedral to its present site on the other side of the River Wear. The school continued to thrive and expand and in the period 1914 to 1918 many 'Dunelmians' went off to serve in the Great War.

Alfred Frederick Maynard was born in 1894 in Durham City and was not only academic, but a fine sportsman too. He left the school in 1912 and went to Cambridge University where he played twice in the Rugby XV against Oxford. In 1913 and 1914 he gained full international honours, playing for England in all the international matches. He graduated with a BA in 1914. He was commissioned as a sub lieutenant in the Royal Naval Volunteer Reserve and was present at the evacuation of Antwerp and at the first raid on the Suez Canal. He was wounded in Gallipoli and, after recovering from his wounds, was in the forefront of the attack by the Royal Naval Division on 13 November, leading the Howe Battalion. He was seen to be killed attempting to get into the German third line position. His body was never identified and his name is on the Thiepval Memorial to the Missing.

A second 'Old Dunelmian' was killed the following day when the Reverend Ernest Wilberforce Trevor, Chaplain to the 13/Rifle Brigade, was killed on 14 November. As A F Maynard entered the school in 1906, so E W Trevor had left in 1905. He too was a fine sportsman and captained both the school cricket and rugby teams before proceeding to Oxford, where he played rugby for the university. He graduated in 1908 and obtained an MA in 1912. He was ordained priest in 1910 and applied for an Army Chaplaincy in 1915. Attached to the Rifle Brigade, he went into action with the 13 Battalion on the morning of 14 November in the assault on the 'Yellow Line' between Beaucourt sur l'Ancre and Beaumont-Hamel. While he was busy assisting the wounded, he was killed by shellfire. He was subsequently found and is buried in Hamel Military Cemetery.

A contemporary of the Reverend E W Trevor at the school was Lieutenant Frank Claggett Caird, 3/Royal Inniskilling Fusiliers. He entered the school in 1904 and left in 1906 and at the outbreak of war was Life Inspector at the London West End Branch of the North British and Mercantile Insurance Company. On 3 August 1914 he joined the Drake Battalion of the Royal Naval Division and was with A F Maynard in Antwerp, the Suez Canal and Gallipoli. At the end of 1915 he was gazetted into 3 Royal Inniskilling Fusiliers and went through heavy fighting on the Somme. As the divisions featured in this book were relieved, so his battalion came forward into the line and on 18 November he was killed in a night attack.

A total of 98 'Old Dunelmians' were killed from a total of 535 who served. The most notable of these was the writer and poet W N Hodgson. He was a contemporary of A F Maynard and played in the same school rugby team but went on to Oxford University where, strangely perhaps for a man of his disposition and wide talent, was very active in the University Officer Training Corps. Hodgson's famous poem *Before Action* immortalises him, but he wrote much more, and there is still a Memorial Essay Prize in his name, a bursary, for the pupil at Durham who writes the best essay each year.

Nowell Oxland was a friend of W N Hodgson and also showed similar talent for the written word. His death in Gallipoli limited his output to one published book of prose and poetry. On hearing of his death Hodgson wrote a poem in his memory. Lieutenant Oxland, 6/Border Regiment, is buried in Green Hill Cemetery, Suvla Bay.

At Green Hill Cemetery Gallipoli. The Grave of Nowell Oxland.

It seems somewhat churlish to pick out any other 'Old Dunelmians' who seem to catch the eye above others. There were other rugby internationals and writers. Captain Arthur James Dingle, 6/East Yorkshire Regiment, played in the same England XV as A F Maynard and was killed on 22 August at Suvla Bay, Gallipoli. His younger brother, Surgeon Hugh John Dingle, Royal

Naval Volunteer Reserve, was killed ten months later.

Two brothers, Rex and Rod Gee, from Sunderland, both served in the Durham Light Infantry. Reginald Claude Moline Gee, the eldest, left the school in 1915 and went straight into the 21/Durham Light Infantry. He survived the battles of the Somme, Arras and Third Ypres and was promoted to captain. He was killed just four days before the end of the war on 7 November 1918. Charles Hilton Rodney Gee, his brother, survived the war. He left the school and joined 9 Durham Light Infantry in 1916. He became adjutant to Brigadier R B Bradford VC, the most decorated of those famous brothers. He returned to go to Cambridge University and teach at Clifton College, Bristol. In 1939 he joined up again and was captured in the retreat to Dunkirk and was a prisoner of war for the duration. Once again, he returned to Clifton College and spent the rest of his life there. I visited him in Bristol just a few years ago where, although over 100 years old, he was quite active and of good recall. He has since died, but remembered W N Hodgson very well, who was Head Boy when he was a junior in 1911. In particular, he remembered him winning the school steeplechase and immediately being violently sick which induced others standing nearby to do likewise! He was still in touch with the Bradford family, whose senior relative, a lady, still holds ownership of all the medals awarded to all the brothers. He also gave me some copies of letters written to him by his brother Rex before he went into action on 1 July 1916 which are very poignant.

One of the very last 'Old Dunelmians' to lose his life was Lance Corporal Herbert Golightly Constantine, 7 Border Regiment. He was born in 1899 and had lived in Cardiff. He went to the school in 1915 and left in July 1917, not yet eighteen years of age. He joined the army immediately and went to France in April 1918. On 1 June he went into action for the first time and was straight away killed. He was still only eighteen years of age.

After the war a new school chapel was planned as a memorial to all those who had died and in 1924 the foundation stone was laid. By 1926 it was dedicated, although there was not enough money to complete it. This was not achieved until 1956. It stands in an elevated position looking down on the main school buildings and with a wonderful view of the fine Norman cathedral.

The school, as with many others of its type, has now become co-educational and each morning the boys and girls mount 98 steps to the chapel to begin the day. Each step represents a life lost in the Great War.

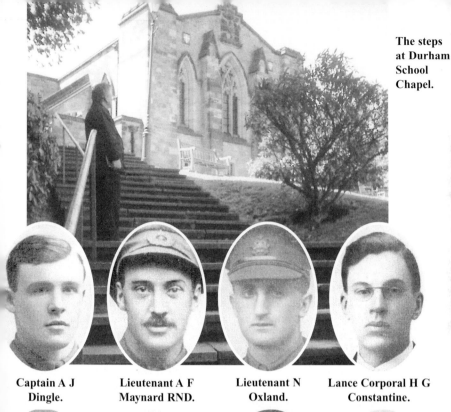

The steps at Durham School Chapel.

Captain A J Dingle.

Lieutenant A F Maynard RND.

Lieutenant N Oxland.

Lance Corporal H G Constantine.

Reverend E W Trevor.

Lieutenant W N Hodgson MC

Lieutenant F C Caird.

Captain C M Gee MC.

And so we passed and others had our place
But well we know that here till days shall cease
While the great stream goes seaward and trees bloom
God's kindness dwells about these courts of peace.

W N Hodgson OD, 1905 -11

Surgeon H J Dingle.

Chapter Twelve

THE CEMETERIES

The Ancre British Cemetery

This cemetery contains the largest concentration of graves from the battles on 1 July, 3 September and 13 November 1916. Several smaller battlefield cemeteries were concentrated here later and details of these are given in the register or can be obtained from the Commonwealth War Graves Commission. One of the most notable graves is that of the son of Lord Rothermere, the Honourable Vere Harmsworth, killed near the redoubt above the cemetery on the right hand side. A second Harmsworth son was also killed in the war. Also buried here is Captain E S Ayre of the Newfoundland Regiment one of four cousins, two sets of brothers, all from the same family, who were killed on 1 July 1916.

Private Willam Laverty, 12/Royal Irish Rifles, is buried here, killed on 1 July 1916. His parents both died in a flu epidemic and; left an orphan, he was taken in by his next door neighbours, Mr and Mrs Huey. Rose Huey was later left alone to bring up her own three boys and William, when her husband also died of flu. When war broke out James Huey, Alex Huey and William all joined up. James was killed at Loos, and Alex and William were together at Hamel, where William was killed. Rose Huey wrote for information concerning William, but received an evasive answer. Alex wrote to his mother, telling her of William's death. Alex was eventually killed at Passchendaele, leaving just one surviving son.

Rose Huey's letter to the war office.

Madam.

If this refers to No. 642 William Laverty of the 12th Bn. ROYAL IRISH RIFLES. No casualty has been reported concerning him and as far as is known he is still serving with his Battalion in France.

In making inquiries the Regiment Battalion and Regtl. Number should always be quoted to facilitate identification.

Thos Williams

For O. i/c. Infantry Records, Dublin

(stamp: RECORD OFFICE 26 JUL. 1916 ... DUBLIN)

Reply sent to Rose Huey.

12/8/1916

Dear Mother

Just a few lines to let you know that I received your letter all right glad to know that you are all well at home as this leaves me in very good health at present I was begining to think that I was never going to get any more letters as it is now about a month since I got any. ~~—~~ Willie is killed so you need not have minded writing to the war office anything about him I feel a bit lonely without him now but not so bad as being with nobody at all the rest of the fellows keeps me from feeling just so bad all at present from your loving son Alex

Alex Huey

Son, Alex's letter to his mother – 'Willie is killed...'

Alex Huey

The Ancre British Cemetery.

In 1996 it was widely reported that electricity workers installing a new sub-station at the cemetery had unearthed four bodies. One was a soldier of the Black Watch, while the other two were from the Worcester Regiment and an Irish Regiment. The last body was too badly burnt to determine his regiment. However, later, when it came to exhume the bodies, the Commonwealth War Graves could find only three, the Irish soldier was not there. The other three were buried in the cemetery on the left just near the entrance, next to an unknown soldier, who was already interred. The following year a substantial wreath from Northern Ireland was laid on the original unknown grave, perhaps mistakenly. The riddle of the 'missing' Irishman has never been solved, but as this book is being written *The Worcester Evening News* is renewing an effort to identify the Worcester soldier and has managed to narrow the search down to ten names.

Hamel Military Cemetery

This cemetery is tucked away and is easily missed. There is no parking area, but a visit will prove worthwhile. It is the burial place for Lieutenant Colonel F J Saunders (Anson) and Lieutenant Colonel N O Burge (Nelson), both commanding officers in the Royal Naval Division. Lieutenant G W Hawkins and Second Lieutenant E C Holmes of the 13/King's Royal Rifle Corps were brought back here after the final attack on Beaucourt village.

Lieutenant Hawkins was probably the first officer into Beaucourt village on the morning of 14 November. He was educated at Alleyne's School, Dulwich and returned from China to enlist. In 1915 he married Caroline who gave birth to a son, just eleven weeks before his death, which is recorded as 15 November. The reason for this discrepency is not clear and was queried by his relatives. The army stated that this was the date he arrived at Hamel when he was found to be already dead.

The Reverend E W Trevor, 13/Royal Fusiliers' Chaplain, also rests here. There are 487 men of the Royal Naval Division, and also other graves from the actions described in this book.

F S Kelly was born in Australia but was educated at Eton and won a music scholarship to Balliol College Oxford. He was a champion oarsman of his time. He rowed for Oxford against Cambridge and was a member of the record breaking Leander crew. Among his many individual achievements, he won the Diamond Sculls at Henley a record three times. He was also a gifted pianist and gave several concerts at notable London venues.

Martinsart Military Cemetery

This is in a very pleasant, rural setting and visitors are often surrounded by the orchestration of many animals, including chickens, goats, sheep and cattle. The headstones are of an unusual red sandstone which was used as an experiment. There are a number of Royal Naval Division graves, including that of Lieutenant Commander F S Kelly DSO of the Hood Battalion, Freyberg's friend and fellow officer.

Also buried here are fourteen men of 13/Royal Irish Rifles who were killed by a stray shell on 28 June 1916. The Commanding Officer of 10/Royal Irish Rifles, Lieutenant Colonel H C Bernard, killed on 1 July is also here.

Varennes Military Cemetery

This cemetery is a little further afield, off the normal 'visitor trail' and is where some of the wounded were brought back. It is a lovely setting and includes a most unusual personal memorial in the form of a large bird bath or animal watering trough given to the memory of E A F Allen, 10/Royal Fusiliers, by his parents. Among the November graves is that of Lieutenant Colonel A S Tetley, commanding officer of the Drake Battalion.

Memorial Trough at Varennes Military Cemetery.

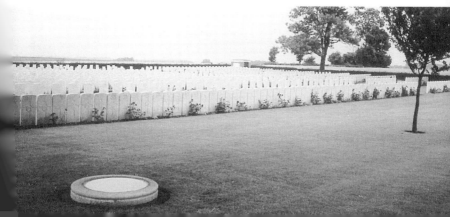

Puchevillers Military Cemetery

As the divisions were relieved, so they took their wounded with them and Puchevillers, on the D11 road to Amiens, is a pleasant and easy drive and the cemetery is quietly tucked away from the main road among the fields. Plot Six contains many graves of men who are buried in date order as they died, some living over a week before succumbing. The longest surviving that I noted was Able Seaman Frank, aged eighteen, who lived for twelve days after the battle.

Puchevillers Military Cemetery.

Knightsbridge Cemetery

This cemetery is difficult to access. It can be seen easily from the entrance to the Newfoundland Memorial Park, but is reached by road and track from Mesnil village.

It is on the site of the communication trenches and various battalion headquarters on the northern end of the divisional sector close to Mary Redan. It contains the graves of eight (all but one) of the officers of 4/Bedfords killed in the November battle. The exception was Second Lieutenant L S Wilkinson, who was evacuated with the other five wounded officers, but who died at Etaples, near Bolougne. Also buried here are all five officers of 10 Royal Dublin Fusiliers killed on 13 November 1916. There are other graves from the actions covered by this book. These include some men of the Royal Naval Division killed before the action on November 13 and 14. I also noticed two, graves of boys aged seventeen years of age who fought with the King's Royal Rifle Corps.

Rifleman A E S Hubbard, 17 KRRC, killed in action 3 September 1916, was buried in Knightsbridge Cemetery.

Second Lieutenant L S Wilkinson, Bedfordshire Regiment, died of wounds later and is the only Bedfords' officer not in Knightsbridge Cemetery.

Knightsbridge Cemetery.

Chapter Thirteen

A SHORT TOUR OF THE SOMME

The visitor going to the Somme battlefields for the first time may be interested to see something of the rest of the area, other than just the part covered by this book. This brief guide starts at the most northerly point of the attack proper, excluding the diversionary attack which was detached at Gommecourt. Go to Serre on the D919 between Arras and Amiens. At the bottom of the hill, south of the village you will find a group of cemeteries and war graves signs. Go up the track beside the farm, signposted to Sheffield Park.

SHEFFIELD MEMORIAL PARK, SERRE

This was the place where several of the northern 'Pals' battalions attacked towards the village of Serre. The memorial park actually stands where the Accrington Pals went over, the Sheffield Pals were further to the right as you stand facing the entrance, and further still in that direction were the Barnsley Pals. If you take a walk that way, along the front of the wood, you will see substantial remains of the actual frontline trench, especially where the undergrowth is not too thick. In places it has been filled with brushwood. To the left, in the open field, was where the Leeds Pals, Bradford Pals, and Durham Pals were located. This area stretches back to the farm and to Serre Number One Cemetery, where many of them are buried at the back.

HAWTHORN CRATER AND SUNKEN ROAD

The single track road opposite the farm follows the German front line position to Beaumont Hamel. Turn right here to visit the crater, the entrance to which, is on the left about 100 metres from the village. A little further on is the Sunken Road, on the right, unchanged since it was filmed full of Lancashire Fusiliers on the morning of the battle. The site of the filming of the explosion at the crater is a bit further on, on the right, about 15 metres to the right of the pumping station as you face the bank, where vestiges of tunnels and trenches can still be seen.The British front line crossed the road exactly where the hard surfaced track known as the Old Beaumont Road joins it and it is easily passable by car for two hundred metres after which it turns sharply to the left and becomes a metalled road leading to the Hawthorn Ridge.

NEWFOUNDLAND PARK

Nearly a hundred acres of preserved trenches can be seen here. There is a visitor centre and guided tours are available.

ULSTER MEMORIAL TOWER

Continue to Hamel village and take the road to Thiepval. The tower stands on the old German front line. There is a visitor centre and Memorial Room. Refreshments can be purchased.

THE THIEPVAL MEMORIAL

The Thiepval Memorial commemorates those who fought in the Battle of the Somme and who have no known grave. It stands high on the ridge and is a landmark which can be seen from many distant vantage points. It was designed by Sir Edwin Lutyens and was dedicated in July 1932 by the Prince of Wales.There are over 73,000 names on the memorial and many of those killed in the battle described in this book are recorded here.

Behind the memorial, as you approach from the main entrance, is a cemetery laid out with French graves on the left and British graves on the right which was created to symbolise the fraternity between the two nations. An annual memorial service is held every year on 1 July at 10 30.am.

The registers are kept in bronze safes at either side of the steps leading up to the altar. In case of difficulty call at the workbase on the left of the entrance and ask for the Thiepval area supervisor or telephone the Commonwealth War Graves Office at Beaurains 0321710324.

Follow the road to Pozieres and turn right towards Albert. At La Boiselle crossroads, turn left and follow the signs to 'La Grande Mine'.

LOCHNAGAR CRATER

This site has been bought privately and put into trust so that it can never suffer the fate of other craters and be filled in. It stands on the German front line and was blown on July 1. Each year on that anniversary a memorial service is held at 7 30.am

TRIPLE TAMBOUR MINES

If you are walking, or have a four wheel drive vehicle, it is possible to carry on past the crater and continue for about a kilometre. Otherwise, go back to the main road and go towards Albert. At the first roundabout, take the by-pass to Amiens. At the next roundabout, turn left towards Peronne. At Fricourt, turn left into the village. Beyond the British cemetery you pass on the left, there is a track between some farm buildings and a house numbered eleven, with a white wall.This leads to the Triple Tambour mines. These were smaller mines and the result of their detonation is obvious.

Coming from the other way you will pass Fricourt New Military Cemetery, with over two hundred burials, of which nearly all are the 10 West Yorkshire Regiment who suffered the most casualties on July 1. In Fricourt village, you will find a German military cemetery. Continue on the road to Contalmaison, where you should turn right at the crossroads, then first left. Follow this single track road until there is a very sharp turn to the left at the bottom of the hill. This will take you to the Red Dragon.

German soldiers at a training camp near Hamburg 1915. Romberg is second right from the Instructor.

Herman Romberg was a Sergeant in the German army who fought in the Beaumont Hamel area in November 1916. A Scottish soldier threw a grenade at him which missed but it landed behind him and severely injured both his legs. He was picked up and taken back to Contay, where British doctors had to amputate both of them. He subsequently died, and is now buried in the Fricourt German Cemetery.

Herman Romberg in a deep German trench.

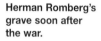

Herman Romberg's grave soon after the war.

38 WELSH DIVISION MEMORIAL

This was erected in 1987 and overlooks the scene of the first attempt to take Mametz Wood on 7 July 1916. On 10 July a heavier attack across ground to the left, as you stand at the dragon, succeeded. The track past the memorial has recently been improved, so it should be possible to drive to the distant Flat Iron Copse Cemetery and on to the road, where you should turn right.

DELVILLE WOOD

At Longueval there is the South African Memorial and Museum. There is a visitor centre and shop which sells books, souvenirs and light refreshments.

Chapter Fourteen

AND AFTERWARDS

The crew made their final checks and adjustments to the Royal Canadian Airforce Wellington bomber as they waited on the runway at Marston Airfield near York. The pilot, Les Lauzon, set his altimeters to nought and the fully laden plane taxied into line awaiting its turn for take off into the twilight. The date was 8 June 1944. Two days previously the Allies had made their assault on the beaches of Normandy and plans had been laid well in advance to ease their progress into occupied France.

The last sortie made by this crew had been to bomb the German batteries on the Normandy coast at Merville. These guns had still been operating prior to the invasion in spite of special attention from His Majesty's Royal Navy. This sortie, though, was to take them further into enemy territory.

The target was to be the railway marshalling yards at Cambrai and, avoiding the heavier 'flak' near Lille, the plane arrived over its target and delivered its payload. Les turned the plane and set off for home. The Luftwaffe, though, had other ideas. Night fighter planes located the attackers and the

Les Lauzon, Royal Canadian Airforce.

Royal Canadian Airforce Wellington was hit by a burst of fire into its port wing. Fire spread rapidly and it was quickly apparent the plane was doomed. The stricken plane started to lose height and evacuation was ordered. One by one, the crew jumped into the darkness below while Les did his best to keep the aircraft stable. Finally there was only one other crew member left, but he refused to jump as there was only one serviceable parachute left between them. It is impossible to imagine what both men must have been thinking and feeling as the plane plunged downwards. Les switched on the emergency channel on the radio only to hear a distressed voice calling for his mother. Eye witnesses below heard and saw the plane on its final descent. It passed low over the village of Hamel and further on over Beaucourt sur l'Ancre. Les could see nothing, but he knew the Vale of York, from where he had taken off, was low lying in relation to sea level and at 300 feet he decided to cut everything and put the plane down. It passed directly over the spire of Miraumont church missing it, seemingly, by inches, missed the houses as well by a similar margin and headed straight for the railway embankment. Complete disaster was imminent but suddenly there was a grinding crash, the aircraft slewed round, changed direction and eventually slid to a halt. The port wing had hit the ground first and completely altered the path of its 'flight.' Both men scrambled out of the plane without as much as a scratch and ran off into the darkness.

Hiding in a ditch near the German airfield at Grévillers, just up the road from Miraumont, the two reflected on their truly miraculous escape, but quickly abandoned plans to steal a German plane and fly back to Britain! At night they hid in a small cow-shed. Hunger forced them to disclose their presence to the French farmer who came each day to tend his cattle. He brought them eggs and wine and later the 'resistance' arrived to question them.

Chief interrogator was an attractive young woman with beautiful, long hair who spoke perfect English. Satisfied as to their credibility, they were given new identities as Frenchmen and lived with families in the village of Hébuterne nearby. Their papers, ID tags and uniforms were hidden behind stones chiselled out of the crypt of a nearby church. There were other 'flyers' similarly 'billeted' in the area, but time dragged on and the allied airmen grew restless. Furthermore, the French families they lived with were naturally nervous of being discovered harbouring enemies of the Reich and so a plan was devised to walk to Paris.

The 'resistance' led them to Albert and through the town out on to the Amiens road. Leading the way in extended file, was Les Lauzon. It was after curfew and a car approached. Realising the danger Les went into a nearby field and pretended to be a farmer examining his crops. The car stopped. It could not have been worse. It was the Gestapo.

Les' experiences in the hands of the Gestapo, first in Amiens prison and then in Lille are not for recording here. He did, however, escape the numerous firing squads and was eventually handed over to the Luftwaffe and, along with other allied prisoners, put on a train bound for prisoner of war camps. Travelling through Germany, the train stopped at a station where an angry crowd had gathered. Feeling was running high over intensive bombing of the German cities and word had got out that there were allied airmen on the train.The Luftwaffe guards and their officers, however, hid the airmen and stood in front of the train's windows, assuring the crowd there were no such prisoners on the train.

Every member of Les Lauzons' Wellington bomber crew survived and returned home to Canada after the war. In 1994 Les revisited the Ancre valley and the village of Miraumont on the fiftieth anniversary of the crash. He met villagers who remembered his amazing escape and who gave him small souvenirs made from the wreckage of his aircraft. No-one could tell him which church his belongings had been hidden in and in all probability remained hidden there. Neither could anyone identify the girl with the long, beautiful hair who spoke perfect English. Perhaps she was English, an SOE agent dropped into France, returning to the UK later.

This brief account is an abridged version of several hours of

All the crew returned to Canada.

conversation I had with Les.

'How old where you when all this happened?' I asked. After a pause, Les reflected, 'I had my twenty first birthday hiding in a ditch at Grévillers.'

Selective Index

Allen Pte. EAF 149
Albany Duke of 139
Annable Pte. W 40,45
Armfeld Pte. 40,45
Aron Sub Lieut. EM RND 60
Astle Pte. H 40,45
Atkinson Capt. TJ 23,25,30

Ball Lieut. BH 40,45
Bartlett Sec.Lieut. EFP 41,45,46
Bastin Capt. E. 70,74
Bearn Lieut. BH 40,45
Bennison Sgt. 28,35
Blacker Lieut. Col. SW 19, 28,30,93
Blunden Lieut. EC MC 42,45,115,140
Bradford Brigadier General RB VC MC 144
Brew Capt. JG 24,30,35
Buckley Pte. 24,35
Burge Lieut. Col. WO 64,74,148

Caird Lieut. FC 143,145
Campbell A Lieut. MC RND 91,93,124
Campbell Lieut. Commdr. PS 67,68,74
Cartwright Lieut. Col. FJW DSO 56,60,62,71,73
Cather Lieut. St.G VC 29,32,93
Constantine L/Cpl. HG 144,145
Coombs Rose 10,13
Cox Lieut. JF MC 71,72,74,118

Dawe Sec. Lieut. AH 88,89
Dewar Lieut. LJA 59
Dicks Pte. WEV 45
Dingle Capt. AJ 143,145
Dingle Surgeon HJ 143,145
Dyett Lieut. ELA RND 92

Edmondson Lieut. CA RND 66
Edwards Lieut. RCG RND 62,74
Elliott Petty Offr. J 63
Ellis Lieut. Commdr. BH DSO 60-62,74

Emerson Lieut. JH 64,74
Ensor Capt. S 23,30,35

Fairweather Pte. A 79
Fish Lieut. SH RND 65,66,74
Fletcher Sub Lieut. CGO 58
Forster Capt. J 69,74
Freyberg Lieut. Col. BC VC 62,65-70,73,85,87-90,93,130

Gamble Rifleman DJ 29,35
Gee Capt. CHR MC 144
Gee L/Cpl. FE 64
Gee RCM 144,145
Gilliland Lieut. Commdr. JM 59,61,67,73
Goldsmith Lieut. FB MC and Bar 40.45
Gow Surgeon CH 60,73
Greene Lieut. GR 35,41,42
Griffiths Capt. J 22,35

Haig Sir Douglas Haigh 37,38,51,52
Harmsworth Lieut. The Hon. VST 62,46
Hart Sub Lieut. AR 66
Haughton Lieut. TG 21,35
Hawkins Sec. Lieut. GW 88,93,130,148
Herbert AP 48,74,115,116
Hinder L/Cpl. G 89,93
Hodgson Lieut. WN MC 143,145
Holmes Sec. Lieut. EC 88,93,148
Hubbard Rifleman AES 150
Huey Pte. A 147
Huey Rose 146,147
Humphreys Sec. Lieut. RG 86,93
Hutchinson Lieut. Col. ARH DSO 57,60,62,71,73

Innes Capt. WR 80,84

Jackson Rifleman EA 41
Jerrold Douglas 7,47,62
Johnston Capt. CM 23,24,30

Kelly Lieut. FS DSO RND 65,66,74,149

Kerr Lieut. W RND 66
Kirk Capt. R 80,84

Laidlaw Petty Offr. R MM 88
Lauzon Les. 154-156
Laverty Pte. W 146
Leach Lieut. TS 40,45
Lemon Lieut. AD 28,29,35,123
Lutyens Sir Edward 13

Macmillan Harold MP 9,10
Martin Sec.Lieut. CW 58
Maynard Lieut. AF RND 58,73,142-145
McCluggage Lieut. W 21,35
McCormack Sgt. JJ 71,72,74
McCracken Surgeon W DSO and Bar 89
McCusker Lieut. P 70,75,76
McMahon Lieut. VM MC 71,74,118
McNaghten Sir EH 21-23,35,110,118
Mullholland L/Cpl. S 25
Montague Capt.The Hon. SL 88-91
Mothe Lieut. CDF de la RND 58,73
Murray Capt.CS 29,55

Norton CSM 10

O'Neill Sec. Lieut. F 70,75,76
Oxland Lieut.N 143,145

Paris Sir Archibald 47
Pemberton Lieut. FS 86,93
Plimpton Capt. RA 81,84
Praagh Lieut. HB van 62,74
Priest Sgt. T 71-72,74

Ramsay-Fairfax Commdr. WG DSO 60,74
Rattigan Capt, CS 69,74
Reddick Sub Lieut. GA 65
Romberg Sgt. H 153

Quigg Pte. R VC 23,94,118

Saunders Lieut. Col. FJ 148

Sewell Lieut. HV RND 61,74
Shute Major General CD 48
Simpson Vic. 99,108,131,132,134
Skinner Capt. FT 40,45
Smith Lieut. Col. EJ StG 70-72,74
Spinney Lieut. KT 39,45
Sterndale Bennett Lieut. Commdr. W 68,74
Stevenson Capt. T 81,84
Stokes Lieut. LM 59
Stocks Capt. J MC 88,89,93,130,131
Stollard Major G 39,40,45
Sweet Rifleman L 89,93

Taffs Cpl. 83,84
Tetley Lieut. Col. AS 67,74,149
Tew Sec.Lieut. 40,40,45
Thornton Rev. SAL 71-73,76,118
Trevor Rev. EW 142,145,148
Trinkle Heinrich 34
Turnbull Pte. J 45

Walmsley Alan 98,99
Walters Capt. HV 39,40,45
Ward Surgeon JS 62,64,74
Ware Sir Fabian 13
Wilson Lieut. Col. LO 62
Worthington Sgt. J 42,45

Place Names
Albert 97,98,99
Auchonvillers Wood 126
Beaucourt-Hamel 11,66
Beaucourt Mill 79
Beaucourt Station 53,62,65,79, 83, 87,127
Beaucourt sur L'Ancre 11,16,17,54, 65,87
Beaumont-Hamel 11,27,38,53,54,57
Beaumont Quarries 119-121
Bloody Road, The 140
Bushmills 110,111
Chalk Pits, The 133
Circus, The 118,119
Commonwealth War Graves Commision 99,100

Corbie 16
Crow's Nest, The 28,68,110, 115,136
Durham School 142
Gordon Trench 38,39,113
Grandcourt 32,33,82
Green Line 53,59,62,65
Hamel 11,27,29,37,54
Hansa Line 32,79,80,82,83,141
Kentish Caves 42,115,116
Mary Redan 19,38,55,109-112,114 115,117
Mill Trench 79,140
New Trench 21,23
Picturedrome, The 68,108,115,135
Popes Nose, The 43,140
Railway Alley 130
Railway Sap 27,123
Red Line 54,92 132
Redoubt Alley 130
Roberts Trench 38,39,113
Schwaben Redoubt, The 24,32,33, 43,78 109,140
Strasburg Line, The 32,43 78 81,140
St Pierre Divion 33,34,80,83,84, 136-140
Station Alley 128,129
Station Road 57,59-61,128,129
Station Trench 53,59,65
Stuff Redoubt 32-34
Stockton-on-Tees 10
Stoneyhurst College 75
Sunken Road, The 111
Triple Tambour Mines 152
Ulster Tower 140,152
Verdun 17
Yellow Line 53,59,60,61,65,66
William Redan 26,109,110,115,135

Divisions
36 (Ulster) Division 16-35
37 Division 51,85-93
39 Division 27,37-46,67,77-84, 114,115
49 (West Riding) Division 35,38-42
63 (Royal Naval) Division 47-76,85-93

Brigades
108 16-35, 106-112
109 32-35
111 51, 85, 129
116 38-42
117 38-42
118 39-42
146 42-43
147 42-43
188 47, 56
189 47
190 47, 68

Battalions
Anson 56,58-62
4   Bedfordshire 58,62,68,69
4/5 Black Watch 39,78-80,84
1/1 Cambridgeshire 67,78-80,84
1/6 Cheshire 78-80
Drake 65-68
1/4 Duke of Wellington's 42,43
1/5 Dukeof Wellingtons's 42,43
14 Hampshire 38-44
Hawke 62-64,68
1/1 Hertfordshire 78,79,82,84
1   Honourable Artillery Company 62, 65,69,87-89
Hood 62,65-69
Howe 53,58-60
17 King's Royal Rifle Corps 39,40
13 King's Royal Rifle Corps 87-90
Nelson 59,64
13 Rifle Brigade 85,86
10 Royal Dublin Fusiliers 62,68-70
7   Royal Fusiliers 62,69
10 Royal Fusiliers 85
13 Royal Fusiliers 85,86
9   Royal Irish Fusiliers 18,20,23, 23,26,27,106-112
12 Royal Irish Rifles 18,20, 23,26,27,106-112
1   Royal Marines 55,56,61,62
2   Royal Marines 56,61,62
11 Royal Sussex 38-42
12 Royal Sussex 38-42
13 Royal Sussex 38-42

16 Sherwood Foresters 78,80-82
17 Sherwood Foresters 39-40
1/6 West Yorkshire 42,43
1/8 West Yorkshire 42,43
14 Worcestershire 66,68,69

Cemeteries and Memorials
38 Division Memorial 153
Ancre British Cemetery 106,107,
    110,146
Connaught Cemetery 140
Delville Wood 153

Fricourt German Cemetery 152,153
Hamel Military Cemetery 148
Knightsbridge Cemetery 150
Lochnagar Crater 152
Mill Road Cemetery 140
Newfoundland Park 141
Puchevillers Military Cemetery 150
Royal Naval Division Memorial
    131,134
Sheffield Memorial Park 151
Thiepval Memorial 152
Varennes Military Cemetery 149

Acknowledgements

During the time that this book has progressed from being a
collection of rough notes to ultimate completion, many people have
contributed to its progress. Sometimes this has been by way of
encouragement and at other times of more specific value, for example,
the loan of a photograph. The list of names here is in no order of merit,
other than as they come to mind and I apologise to anyone missing
from the list who should warrant inclusion, it is simply that memory
fails over a period of time.

Robert Thompson; Kyle Tallett;Tony Froome; Sean Joyce; Sue Cox;
Charles Haskell; Joe and Hannah Williams; Brian Lee; Rose Pugh (nee
Hubbard); Peter Rodway; Michael Monaghan; Alexander Thompson;
Sandra Gibson; Clive Bowery; Ursi Maier; David Tillotson; Trevor
Tasker; Frances Willmoth; Michael Speakman, who accompanied my
wife, Julie, on the search for the tank pits, and got bogged down in the
mud, and had to be rescued by Derek Heaney, (with four wheeled-drive
vehicle). Emma Renshaw; Helen Renshaw; Nigel Cave, who had to
weed out all the mistakes, and to Paul Wilkinson, who then somehow
designed and produced the finished product from the red markings on
the proof!

Among the organisations that I should mention; The Archdiocese of
Glasgow, Durham School, Stoneyhurst College, Oakham School.